National Park

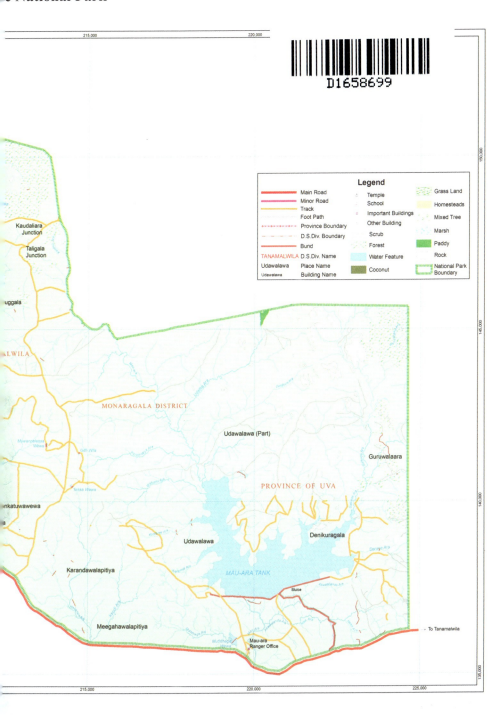

A Pictorial Guide to
Uda Walawe National Park

A Pictorial Guide to
Uda Walawe National Park

Edited by
Sarath Kotagama

Field Ornithology Group of Sri Lanka
Depatment of Zoology, University of Colombo,
Colombo 03.

A Pictorial Guide to
Uda Walawe National Park
Edited by
Sarath Kotagama

© 2014 Field Ornithology Group of Sri Lanka

All rights reserved. No part of this book may be reproduced or transmitted in any form or by any means, electronic or mechanical, including photocopy, recording or any information retrieval system without the prior written permission of the copyright holder.

ISBN 978-955-8576-33-5

Typography, Layout and Graphic:
Indrika Kaggoda Arachchi

Published by:
Field Ornithology Group of Sri Lanka, in collaboration with Dilmah Conservation.

Field Ornithology Group of Sri Lanka	Dilmah Conservation
Department of Zoology,	111, Negombo Road,
University of Colombo,	Peliyagoda,
Colombo 3, Sri Lanka.	Sri Lanka.

Assisted by:

Department of Wildlife Conservation
811A, Jayanthipura,
Battaramulla,
Sri Lanka.

Front cover,
Asian Elephant
© Namal Kamalgoda

Back cover,
Chestnut-headed Bee-eater
© Izabela Urbaniak

Printed with VOC free, non toxic vegetable oil-based environmentally-friendly ink, printed on FSC™ certified paper eliminating fiber from high conservation value forests and controversial sources.

Printed by:
Gunaratne Offset (Pvt) Ltd

Contributors

Plants
Photographs: Nalinda Peiris, Kusum Fernando & Meauranga Perera
Text: Meauranga Perera

Molluscs
Based on: A Guide to the Freshwater Fauna of Ceylon & T.G.M. Priyadarshana
Illustrations & Photographs: An Illustrated Guide to the Land Snails of Sri Lanka Natural Forest and Cultivated Habitats & T.G.M. Priyadarshana

Arthropoda
Photographs & Illustrations: Internet Photographs & A Guide to the Freshwater Fauna of Ceylon
Based on: A Guide to the Freshwater Fauna of Ceylon
Text: Sarath Kotagama

Dung Beetles
Photographs: Enoka P. Kudavidanage
Text: Enoka P. Kudavidanage

Spiders
Illustrations: Kasun de Alwis & Kasun Dayananda
Text: Kasun Dayananda

Dragonflies
Photographs: Amila Sumanapala, Kasun Dayananda, Divanka Randula & Varanga de Silva
Text: Amila Sumanapala

Butterflies
Photographs & Illustrations: Himesh Jayasinhe & Sarath Rajapaksha
Text: Kasun Dayananda, Sarath Rajapaksha & M.D.P. Samarasinghe

Fishes
Illustrations & Photographs: Sampath de A. Goonatilake
Text: Sampath de A. Goonatilake & Shamila Corea

Frogs
Illustrations: Pruthiviraj Fernando
Text: Kelum Manamendra Arachchi

Reptiles
Photographs: Dushantha Kandambi, Dulan Ranga
Text: Sarath Kotagama & Kelum Manamendra Arachchi

Birds
Illustrations: Pruthiviraj Fernando, Kelum Gunasekara, Sarath Kotagama & Gamini Ratnavira
Text: Sarath Kotagama

Mammals
Illustrations: Gamini Ratnavira
Text: Sarath Kotagama & Sampath de A. Goonatilake

Other Photographs
Kusum Fernando, Indrika Kaggoda Arachchi, Rohitha Gunawardena

Massage from the Director General of Wildlife Conservation

Uda Walawe National Park came to being as a result of a major irrigation development scheme in southern Sri Lanka. The prime objectives of its proclamation were two-fold, firstly to protect the catchment area of the Uda Walawe Reservoir and, secondly, to provide habitat for displaced wildlife and offer safe refuge for them within a conservation context.

The geographic location of the Park is strategic in that it is an ecological corridor that connects the Bogahapitiya Forest Reserve with the Yala National Park complex, affording wildlife an array of habitats. The Asian Elephant, as a flagship species in Sri Lanka, has been given special consideration by the Park administration and, as a consequence, visitors are able to see large aggregations of elephants throughout the year.

Managing the Park habitats for large numbers of mega-herbivores facilitates the conservation of other wildlife and promotes ecosystem diversity. The wealth of wildlife in the Park is a tourist draw and income from this attraction contributes not only to the national income but also to local social and economic development.

Today there is pressure on all conservation areas in Sri Lanka owing to the increasing demand for natural resources to fulfill human needs. There is also the necessity to harmonize conservation priorities with accelerated large scale national development projects. The Department of Wildlife Conservation has recognized that the best way to achieve conservation targets is to pursue community-centred conservation strategies; these are both effective and sustainable.

Creating awareness amongst citizens of the value of our natural resources is a first but essential step towards a successful implementation of conservation objectives. We need to create interest in the biological riches of protected areas and encourage the pursuit of scientific knowledge. It is this knowledge that necessarily drives conservation priorities and strategies. This book, which looks at the biological resources of Uda Walawe National Park in a comprehensive way, is an excellent tool to achieve these goals.

The Department is grateful to Dilmah Conservation, a private entity, for providing funds to produce this publication. The research for the book, the artwork, and the photographs were through the efforts of the Field Ornithology Group of Sri Lanka (FOGSL) and the excellence of the design and production is a reflection of the group's values. This book will be an essential guide to all visitors to Uda Walawe National Park and it will enrich their experience.

H.D. Ratnayake
Director General of Wildlife Conservation.

Massage from Dilmah Founder

Dilmah Conservation was founded as an extension of Dilmah's commitment to support sustainable environmental and social development initiatives driven by the guiding principle 'business as a matter of human service'. Since its inception in 2007, Dilmah Conservation has actively engaged in supporting numerous projects dedicated to the conservation and protection of Sri Lanka's rich natural and cultural heritage, the empowerment of indigenous communities, endorsing sustainable livelihood and development practices and promoting environmental education.

As a part of its effort to foster a sense of collective social and environmental responsibility through awareness and education, Dilmah Conservation is pleased to work with the Field Ornithology Group of Sri Lanka (FOGSL) in publishing A Pictorial Guide to Uda Walawe National Park, produced in partnership with the Department of Wildlife Conservation.

The Uda Walawe National Park is an important Protected Area that is home to a variety of plant and animal species, including not only the elephants, leopards and deer that the reserve is famed for, but also rare migratory and endemic birds, and a rich array of insects, reptiles, amphibians and fish. This comprehensive pictorial guide spearheaded by Professor Sarath W. Kotagama provides an excellent overview of the Park's rich floral and faunal diversity, and is geared towards helping both visitors and those interested in additional information on the numerous species found within the Uda Walawe National Park.

Raising awareness on biodiversity and its importance is essential towards ensuring its conservation. This is especially important to cultivate interest and encourage a sense of shared responsibility towards the protection of habitats and ecosystems, and mitigating detrimental practices that hinder conservation. As such, Dilmah Conservation is proud to be part of this pictorial guide as it is a valuable initiative aimed at helping a wider audience improve their understanding of Uda Walawe.

We have pioneered a comprehensive commitment to minimising our impact on the planet, fostering respect for the environment and ensuring its protection by encouraging a harmonious coexistence of man and nature.

Merrill J. Fernando,
Founder of Dilmah

Dilmah Conservation
111, Negombo Road, Peliyagoda, Sri Lanka.
Tel: +94 11 482 2000 Fax: + 94 11 482 2001
E-mail: info@dilmahconservation.org
Web: www.dilmahconservation.org

Preface

Uda Walawe National Park was declared on June 20th, 1972 at a ceremony presided over by the then Minister of Shipping and Tourism, P.B.G. Kalugalle. Proudly standing by was S.D. Saparamadu, the Director of Wildlife Conservation, who had pushed hard for the establishment of the park, along with luminaries such as E.B. Wickramanayake, Barnes Ratwatte, and the President of the Wildlife Protection Society. The birth was not easy. Opposition from land-hungry settlers was fierce. The local MP reflected the views of his constituents. Eventually, though, political opposition was turned around and the settlers provided alternative land.

The extent of land that demarcates the Park stands at 32,315ha (323.15km²). This area contains the Uda Walawe Reservoir and the Mau Aru Reservoir both of which came into being by damming the eponymous rivers. From the outset, Uda Walawe National Park was seen as an ideal refuge for elephants. Year-round water, lush green vegetation, extensive secondary growth, scattered remains of old chena fields, and vast areas of tall grass makes the Park an optimal habitat for the great beasts. But there are many other species of interest, too, both fauna and flora, as this guide will show.

There are thought to be over 300 elephants ranging freely within the Uda Walawe National Park. Their concentration and visibility, in turn, draw human visitors by the thousands. The intent of this book is to enrich the experience of these visitors. All the fauna and flora likely to be seen by those touring the Park are illustrated. This holistic approach is a first for Sri Lanka's national parks and its execution, collating the information from numerous sources, is a noteworthy achievement. It goes without saying that similar guides are planned for Sri Lanka's other national parks.

I hope that visitors to Uda Walawe National Park who use this book will feel enriched as a result.

Sarath Kotagama
Department of Zoology, University of Colombo.

Acknowledgements

The initial intent when planning for this guide was to focus on the larger mammals and birds. It soon became clear, however, that such a publication would be far more meaningful if there were images of the vegetation that the animals ate or roosted upon, and of the other fauna that visitors may happen to come across.

The compilers of this book made a concerted effort to ensure that the illustrations were appropriate for a field guide and the appended text useful. Some of the artwork was already available; missing material was either re-drawn or adapted from the public domain. Hence some of the illustrations may not be of the highest quality.

The role of the layout person is critical because the appearance of the book and, in a field guide, its utility, depends on proper artistic choices. As usual, it was Indrika Kaggoda Aarachchi who fulfilled that role at FOGSL; my thanks to him.

I would like to express my gratitude to Dilmah Conservation for funding the publication of this volume and my thanks to Asanka Abeyakoon and Dilhan Fernando for their encouragement. Their persistence paid off. Asoka Yapa, who was present in my office to assist in laying out his book on the mammals of Sri Lanka, kindly agreed to take a look at the text. Despite the very limited time he had he improved the text considerably. I take full responsibility for any faults that remain.

Sarath Kotagama
Department of Zoology, University of Colombo.

Abbreviations, Symbols & Definitions

Ad.	Adult
BL	Body length
Br.	Breeding plumage
BrR.	Breeding resident
HB	Head and body length
Juv.	Juvenile
NBr.	Non-breeding plumage
SVL	Snout-vent length
TL	Tail length
🟢	Endemic
🟠	Proposed endemic
⬤	Exotic
♀	Female
♂	Male

Contents

Abbreviations, Symbols & Definitions XII

Uda Walawe National Park 17
Physical Features 19
- Geology 19
- Soils 20
- Climate 20

Flora 20
- Dry-Mixed Evergreen Forest 21
- Riverine Forest 22
- Scrub 22
- Grassland 22

Fauna 23
- Fish 23
- Amphibians 24
- Reptiles 25
- Birds 25
- Mammals 26

Illustrations 29
- Plants 31
- Molluscs 67
- Arthropoda 73
- Dung beetles 85
- Spiders 89
- Dragonflies & Damselflies 97
- Butterflies 109
- Fishes 133
- Amphibians 147
- Reptiles 153
- Birds 167
- Mammals 231

References 251

Index 257
- Index of Plants 258
- Index of Molluscs 260
- Index of Arthropoda 261
- Index of Dung beetles 262
- Index of Spiders 263
- Index of Dragonflies & Damselflies 264
- Index of Butterflies 265
- Index of Fishes 268
- Index of Amphibians 269
- Index of Reptiles 270
- Index of Birds 271
- Index of Mammals 276

Checklists 279
- Checklists of Plants 280
- Checklists of Molluscs 285
- Checklists of Arthropoda 286
- Checklists of Dung beetles 288
- Checklists of Spiders 289
- Checklists of Dragonflies & Damselflies 291
- Checklists of Butterflies 292
- Checklists of Fishes 296
- Checklists of Amphibians 298
- Checklists of Reptiles 299
- Checklists of Birds 301
- Checklists of Mammals 310

Uda Walawe National Park

Uda Walawe National Park was declared on 30 June 1972 (Government Gazette Notification No. 14). This was done at the end of the Udawalawe Reservoir Development project. The primary objective of this declaration was to protect the immediate catchment and create a refuge for elephants displaced as a result of the Walawe Basin Development project. A second reservoir, Mau Ara Tank, was constructed inside the park between 1991 and 1998. The Uda Walawe Park is in a strategic location, connecting Lunugumvehera National Park in the south east with Kalthota, Bogahapattiya pond reserve with Koslanda, and Haldummulla in the North.

The total extent of the National Park is 32,315ha, including the Walalwe reservoir, which accounts for 3,405ha at full capacity.

Its western half, on the left bank of the Uda Walawe Reservoir, lies in the Ratnapura District and its eastern sector on the right bank is in the Moneragala District. The southern boundary is defined by the Uda Walawe–Thanamalvila road. To the south of this road is the Sevanagala sugar plantation.

Physical Features

Uda Walawe National Park encompasses the two major drainage basins of the Walawe River and Mau Ara. The enclosed land is an undulating plain at about 100m in elevation, rising to 373m at the foothills of Ulgala in the west. The most prominent feature is the Kalthota Escarpment to the north of the park.

Geology

A large part of Uda Walawe lies within the Vijayan Series, comprising hard crystalline rocks of the pre-Cambrian era. The western and northern boundaries are closer to the transition zone with the Highland or Khondalite Series. Thus, much of the Park is occupied by a variety of gneisses and granites, with extensive exposure of basement rocks in its north-west and eastern sections (Pathirana, 1980).

Soils

Soils in the Park have been developed from residual and alluvial parent materials. They include reddish brown earths, low humic clays, solodized solonetz, and alluvial soils of variable texture and drainage.

Climate

The park location in the Dry Zone is characterized by uniformly high temperatures and seasonal rainfall. Mean annual rainfall is about 1500mm. Rainfall peaks coincide with the Southwest Monsoon in April-May and Northeast Monsoon in October-November. Mean annual temperature is about 32^0C; relative humidity ranges from 61% to 94% in the daytime.

Flora

The Park lies within Floristic Region II of Ashton and Gunatillake (1987). The major vegetation types are Dry-Mixed Evergreen Forest, Riverine Forest along the Walawe River, Savanna, Scrub, Grassland, and some forest plantations of *Eucalyptus* and teak. Most of the teak and *Eucalyptus* plantations have been destroyed by elephants. They began to feed on the bark and subsequently on the flush from around 1998. More than 80% of the area was under forest cover in 1956 but this had declined to 4% by the time the Park was established in 1972. Human habitation, chena cultivation, and removal of vegetation during reservoir construction were the causes of denudation. Very little original vegetation remains. The result is a mosaic of terrestrial and aquatic habitats, including extensive grasslands.

A total of 218 species of vascular plants were inventoried during the Biodiversity Baseline Survey (2006- 07), of which nine species are endemic and six are nationally threatened.

Dry-Mixed Evergreen Forest

The extant closed-canopy forest has a height not exceeding 30m. The tallest emergent canopy tree is Palu (*Manilakara hexandra*) which is scattered throughout the Park. Two tree communities have been recognized in this forest. They are widely distributed but fragmented *Manilkara-Drypetes-Chloroxylon* (Palu-Weera-Burutha) community and *Alseodaphne-Berrya-Diospyros* (Wewarana-Halmilla-Kaluwara) found close to the river and drainage areas.

Other common canopy species are *Cassine glauca, Chloroxylon swietenia, Diospyros ebenum, Drypetes sepiaria, Ficus benghalensis, Holoptelea integrifolia, Pterospermum suberifolium, Schleichera oleosa, Sterculia foetida, Syzygium cumini* and *Vitex altissima*.

Sub-canopy species include *Cassia fistula, Drypetes sepiaria, Diospyros ovalifolia, Cordia dichotoma, Garcinia spicata, Lepisanthes tetraphylla, Pleurostylia opposite* and *Psydrax dicoccos*.

Understorey species include *Capparis zeylanica, Croton officinalis, Clausena indica, Dimorphocalyx glabellus, Erythroxylum zeylanicum, Glycosmis mauritiana, Mallotus rhamnifolius, Micromelum minutum, Miliusa indica, Murraya paniculata, Salacia reticulate, Tarenna asiatica* and *Polyalthia korinti*.

Much of the forest in the park is actually secondary degraded or disturbed areas of Dry-Mixed Evergreen Forest.

Riverine Forest

Riverine Forest (47.0ha, 0.15% of total area) is found along the banks of the Walawe River. The characteristic tree species is *Hopea cordifolia* (Uva Mandora), an endemic and threatened tree species with a threatened endemic height of 35 m. It is the only known Dipterocarp in the Dry Zone. Associated species include: Thimbiri (*Diospyros malabarica*), *Garcinia spicata*, Kolon (*Haldina cordifolia*), Makulla (*Hydnocarpus venenata*), Mee (*Madhuka longifolia*) and Kumbuk (*Terminalia arjuna*). The riverbanks are lined with Kumbuk trees.

Scrub

The area covered by scrub is around 15,800ha or over 50.4% of the total. It is 2-3m in height and occurs in areas of degraded climax and thorn forest. Two main types of scrub are present: i.e., one dominated by mixed indigenous species and a second dominated by the invasive exotic *Lantana camara*.

Commonest species in this habitat are *Acacia leucophloea, Asparagus racemosus, Azadirachta indica, Bauhinia racemosa, Benkara malabarica, Carissa spinarum, Carmona retusa, Catunaregam spinosa, Croton laccifer, Dichrostachys cinerea, Eupatorium odoratum, Flueggea leucopyrus, Lantana camara, Phyllanthus polyphyllus, Scutia myrtina, Streblus asper, Toddalia asiatica,* and *Ziziphus oenoplia.*

Grassland

Grasslands cover around 9,939.3ha, which is about 31.7% of total park area. Grassland has become established in areas of abandoned shifting/chena cultivation that were originally Dry-Mixed Evergreen Forest. *Panicum maximum* (Guinea grass) is dominant with some scattered shrubs and isolated trees.

Recent GIS analytical maps confirm the existence of the major habitat types described above. The remainder consists of *Eucalyptus* plantations (13.5ha, 0.04%), rock outcrops (310.4ha, 1.0%), savanna (3.7ha, <0.1%), abandoned chena (265.5ha, 0.9%), bund (4.90ha, <0.1%), and water (3690.2ha, 11.8%) out of a total area of 31,364.3 ha. Note that this total area is different to the gazetted area of 32,315ha .

Fauna

Udawalawe, with its diverse habitat types, is populated by a diverse vertebrate and invertebrate fauna. The latter is not well documented except for the butterflies.

Fish

The Uda Walawe National Park contains a rich assemblage of fish, representing 25 (30%) of the 82 indigenous species (nine families, 21 genera). However, the number of endemics in the park is low (5 species), representing only 11% of the national total of 44 species. The number of exotic species is relatively high (7 species), accounting for 22% of the total number of species recorded in the Park. The exotic species are mostly confined to the Uda Walawe Reservoir and other tanks but *Oreochromis niloticus* is widespread in the Walawe River and both *O. mossambicus* and *Catla catla* are also present in streams. No nationally threatened species have been recorded.

The following facts are noteworthy:

▲ The most abundant family is the Cyprinidae and the commonest genus is *Puntius,* within the same family Cyprinidae. Of the seven species of *Puntius,* two are endemic.

▲ The most widely distributed species are *Puntius sarana,* the endemic *P. singhala,* and the exotic *Oreochromis niloticus,* all of which occur in the river, streams, the Uda Walawe Reservoir and other tanks but not in the waterholes or ponds.

▲ Only two species were recorded in waterholes and ponds, *Puntius chola* and *P. dorsalis.*

▲ Seven exotic species were recorded in the Uda Walawe Reservoir, of which three were recorded elsewhere. Of the eight indigenous species found in the reservoir, only *Puntius sarana* and *Labeo dussumieri* were as abundant as the exotic species.

The large number of exotic species in the reservoir and other water bodies in the National Park is due to the activities of the Uda Walawe Freshwater Fish Breeding Station of the Ministry of Fisheries. This Station has been stocking water bodies in the area, especially the Uda Walawe Reservoir, with carp and tilapia fingerlings over the years. There are reports of the introduced carp reproducing in Uda Walawe Reservoir. These exotic fish species, particularly those in the Reservoir, contribute significantly to the local fishing industry.

Amphibians

Fifteen species of amphibians, including four endemics and five new species, are known from the park.

Significant findings:

▲ Uda Walawe National Park is important for the conservation of herpetofauna, evident from its relative wealth of species for a site that lies in the Dry Zone. This includes one amphibian genus (*Philautus*) endemic to Sri Lanka.

▲ Species diversity for amphibians was highest in Riverine Forest and lowest in Scrub and Grassland.

Reptiles

26 species of reptiles, including eight endemics, have been recorded from the park.

Other interesting facts about the reptiles are:

▲ The Painted-lip Lizard (*Calotes ceylonensis*) and Lowland Kangaroo Lizard (*Otocryptis nigristigma*), both endemic, are recorded sympatrically in undisturbed and disturbed Dry-Mixed Evergreen Forest.

▲ The endemic and nocturnal Kandyan Gecko *Hemidactylus depressus* and the endemic Day Gecko (*Cnemaspis* sp.) are present.

▲ Two endemic genera of reptiles occur, namely *Lankascincus* and *Nessia*. The relict genus *Nessia* is represented by an unidentified species which could be new to science.

▲ The endemic Tammanna Skink (*Eutropis tammanna*), a new record for Uda Walawe, is recorded in undisturbed Dry-Mixed Evergreen Forest and Grassland with native grass species such as illuk (*Imperata* sp.).

▲ A new record of the rare colubrid snake *Boiga beddomei* in Uda Walawe also represents an extension to the known geographical range of this species. The endemic and nationally vulnerable striped flying snake (*Chrysopelea taprobanica*) is recorded from disturbed Dry-Mixed Evergreen Forest. Other rare species include the Rock Python (*Python molurus*) and the Trinket Snake (*Coeloganthus helena*).

The diversity for reptiles is highest in undisturbed Dry-Mixed Evergreen Forest, intermediate in Grassland, and lowest in Scrub.

Birds

A total of 225 bird species have been recorded in the Park. This includes four endemics and three nationally threatened species, including the critically endangered Rock Pigeon (*Columba livia*). Of these species, 191 are illustrated in the present volume.

Highest species richness is recorded in Grassland, followed by undisturbed Dry-Mixed Evergreen Forest and Riverine Forest while the lowest species richness is recorded in the Scrub habitat. The species richness in Grassland is inflated because of the numerous shallow bodies of water scattered in that habitat.

Of Sri Lanka's 220 breeding resident birds, 61% are thus commonly found within the Park. Endemics (15%) are relatively low in number compared to protected areas in the Wet Zone; this is generally the expected result for Dry Zone sites. Only about 10% of Sri Lanka's 110 migratory species are present, but this is likely an underestimate. The riverine vegetation is known to harbour the elusive Red-faced Malkoha. The first authentic nest of that species in recent years was recorded here in 1976. Scattered forest patches, especially along stream beds and around tanks are good habitats for birds.

Mammals

Forty two (42) species of mammals are known from the park. The following interesting facts should be noted:

▲ Mammals recorded at Uda Walawe belong to 25 genera and 16 families. They comprise several bat species, a dozen rodents including four species of squirrels, the Porcupine (*Hystrix indica*), at least seven species of rats, the Leopard (*Panthera pardus*), the Jungle Cat (*Felis chaus*), three civets, three mongoose species, the Otter (*Lutra lutra*), the Golden Jackal (*Canis aureus*), six species of ungulates, three primates, the Black-naped Hare (*Lepus nigricollis*), and Asian Elephant (*Elephas maximus*).

▲ Six species are endemic, namely Purple-faced Langur (*Semnopithecus vetulus*), Toque Monkey (*Macaca sinica*), Flame-striped Jungle Squirrel (*Funambulus layardi*), Sri Lanka Spiny Mouse (*Mus fernandoni*), White-spotted Chevrotain (*Moschiola meminna*), and Sri Lankan Golden Striped-backed Palm Civet (*Paradoxurus stenocephalus*). One species, the Buffalo (*Bubalus arnee*) is an exotic. The most common species in the Park are the Toque Macaque, the Grey Langur (*Semnopithecus priam*), Spotted Deer (*Axis axis*), Asian Elephant, the Black Rat (*Rattus rattus*), and Wild Boar (*Sus scrofa*).

▲ Eleven species are nationally threatened, of which the endemic Sri Lanka spiny mouse (*Mus fernandoni*) is Critically Endangered.

▲ Species richness for mammals is highest in the Grassland and undisturbed Dry-Mixed Evergreen Forest habitats. This is attributed, at least partly, to the shade and cover afforded by such habitats, particularly the tall grasses.

▲ Udawalawe is renowned for its large Asian Elephant population. It attracts large numbers of visitors because elephants can be easily viewed, especially in the open Grassland habitat.

▲ The Park is probably the best place in Sri Lanka to view the elusive Jungle Cat (*Felis chaus*). These cats can sometimes be glimpsed on the roads at all times of day and night.

▲ Several small mammals are also seen often in the park. Among them are Antelope Rat (*Tatera indica*), Common Rat (*Rattus rattus*), Soft-furred Metad (*Millardia meltada*), White-tailed Wood Rat (*Madromys blanfordi*), Sri Lanka Spiny Mouse (*Mus fernandoni*), Indian Field Mouse (*Mus booduga*), and Painted Bat (*Kerivoula picta*).

Illustrations

Plants
(Plates 1-34)

Flowering plants are a group of vascular plants with their seeds enclosed in fruits. The characteristic feature is the flower, which is a shoot system modified for reproduction.

Angiosperms are by far the most diverse and successful plant group, containing over 95% of all land plant species alive today. These grow in every habitable region and dominate most terrestrial and even some aquatic ecosystems. They represent the majority of economically important plants.

There are 4143 known flowering plants in Sri Lanka representing 214 families and 1522 genera. Of the total number, 75% are indigenous (that is, not introduced by humans) and, of them, approximately 27% are endemic. The number of flowering plants in the Udawalawe National Park area is yet to be fully assessed; a baseline survey was conducted in 2007.

Plate 1

1. *Barleria prionitis*
Porcupine flower
කටු කරඳ, කටු කරඬු
1.75m. Prickly shrub. Much branched.

Leaf: Decussate

Ovate-elliptic-obovate

Tip: Mucronate
Base: Acuminate, tapering
Margin: Entire

Flowers: Large, solitary, corolla: salver-shaped, bright orange yellow

Fruit: Ovoid-oblong capsule

2. *Stenosiphonium cordifolium*
බූ නෙළු, නෙළු
Up to 1.5m. Much branched. Leaf cottony beneath when young.

Leaf: Opposite

Ovate-elliptic

Tip: Acuminate
Base: Cuneate
Margin: Crenate-serrate
Inflorescence: Panicle

Florets: Corolla - funnel-shaped, bluish violet, dark blue dots on the base of corolla lobes

Fruitlet: Linear-oblong capsule

3. *Crinum defixum*
හීන් තොලබෝ
Bulb narrowed above into a cylindrical false stem.

Leaf: Spiral, deeply channelled above, stiff

Linear

Tip: Attenuate
Base: Obtuse/acute
Margin: Short distantly placed teeth present
Inflorescence: 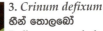 Umbel

Florets: Salver-shaped, perianth tube purplish proximally, green middle, white or purplish distally

Fruitlet: Ovoid or subglobose capsule

PLATE 2

1. *Mangifera zeylanica* 🟢
ඇටඹ, වල් අඹ
Large tree.

Leaf: Spiral

Lanceolate/ovate-oblong

Tip: Rounded, retuse, acute in saplings
Base: Attenuate-cuneate, tapering
Margin: Entire
Inflorescence: Panicle
Florets: Petals as twice as long as sepals, obtuse, clawed and reflexed
Fruitlet: Ovoid drupe

2. *Polyalthia korinti*
මී වැන්න, උල් කෙන්ද
0.7-5m. Slender treelet. Leafy branches pubescent with yellowish hairs when young.

Leaf: Distichous

Elliptic-ovate-lanceolate

Tip: Acuminate
Base: Acute-obtuse
Margin: Entire
Flowers: Solitary, green, petals turn blackish when dry, inner petals longer and more white
Fruit: Globose. Ripen fruit bright crimson, succulent, carpels densely pubescent

3. *Carissa spinarum*
හීන් කරඹ
Intricately branched, scandent tree.

Leaf: Opposite

Ovate/rhomboid

Tip: Acute, apiculate
Base: Acute/rounded
Margin: Entire
Flowers: Scentless, white, rotate corolla
Fruit: Berry black when ripe

1. *Phoenix pusilla*
ඉඳි

Armed palm. Leaf bases & scars on stem. Leaflet joint with rachis marked by a yellow orange pulvinus.

Leaf: Induplicately pinnate, spiral

Leaflet: Elongate-spathulate

Florets: Creamy white when fresh

Fruitlet: Ovoid nut, epicarp-deep red, dark-purple when ripe

Tip: Sharp needle-like apices

Margin: Entire

Inflorescence: Emergence-enclosed in pale green prophyll, covered with pale orange tomentum, later-woody Panicle

---

2. *Calotropis gigantea*
එළ වරා, හෙළ වරා, වරා

Shrubby treelet, young stems and inflorescences pubescent, latex present.

Leaf: Decussate, cottony hairs when young

Obovate

Florets: Corolla-rotate, pale violet or occasionally pure white in the genus

Fruit: Follicle

Tip: Acute-rounded **Base:** Cordate **Margin:** Entire **Inflorescence:** Cyme

---

3. *Wattakaka volubilis*
Green Milkweed climber
අඟුණ, අනුක්කෝල, කිරි අඟුණ, තිත්ත අඟුණ

Climber.

Leaf: Decussate

Ovate-cordate

Florets: Corolla-rotate, green.

Fruitlet: Ovoid-oblong brownish follicle

Tip: Acute-acuminate **Base:** Obtuse, truncate/shallowly cordate **Margin:** Entire **Inflorescence:** Umbel

PLATE 4

1. *Carmona retusa*
හීන් තඹල
Up to 2m. Shrubs or small trees.

Leaf: Fasciculate, rough above

Obvate, oblong, spathulate

Tip: Retuse or 2-7 teeth
Base: Attenuate
Margin: Entire-crenulate
Florets: Corolla salver shaped, white stamens are exerted
Fruitlet: Green, globose drupaceous, ripening brownish

---

2. *Ehretia laevis*
Up to 8m. Shrub or small tree.

Leaf: Distichous

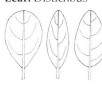

Obovate-elliptic-ovate

Tip: Acute or obtuse
Base: Acute-cuneate
Margin: Entire
Inflorescence: Panicle
Florets: Corolla-salver shaped, white, stamens exserted
Fruitlet: Drupaceous, orange red at maturity

---

3. *Crateva adansonii*
Garlic pear tree
ලුණු වරණ
3-12m. Tree.

Leaf: Trifoliolate, laterals asymmetric, spiral

Leaflet: Elliptic-lanceolate

Tip: Acuminate
Base: Acute
Margin: Entire
Inflorescence: Corymb
Florets: Corolla-rotate, white/ cream/ yellow. Long stamens
Fruitlet: Globose, orange

A Pictorial Guide to Uda Walawe National Park

1. *Gloriosa superba*
නියගලා
Climbing herb.

Leaf: Spiral, sessile.

Lanceolate

Flower: Green changing yellow to red. Narrowly elliptic, strongly crisped, undulate, rotate corolla

Fruit: Oblong capsule

Tip: With tendril
Base: Rounded, cordate/amplexicaul
Margin: Entire

---

2. *Terminalia arjuna*

Up to 25m. Tall tree.

Leaf: Opposite / subopposite, reddish with age

Lanceolate-ovate-oblong

Florets: Corolla-rotate shaped, creamish-greenish white

Fruitlet: Winged drupe

Tip: Obtuse, rounded, apiculate, mucronate
Base: Truncate, rounded
Margin: Crenate
Inflorescence: Panicle

---

3. *Connarus monocarpus*
රදලිය
5m. Scandent shrub. Leaf scars prominent.

Leaf: Imparipinnale

Leaflet: Ovate-oblong

Florets: Corolla-salver shaped, white

Inflorescence: Paniculate cymes

Fruit: Irregularly obovoid, fusiform follicle. Green through yellow to scarlet red

Tip: Subacuminate-caudate & twisted
Base: Obtuse, rounded
Margin: Entire

PLATE 6

1. *Argyreia osyrensis*
දුම්බද
Liana. Stem has dense whitish indumenta.

Leaf: 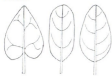 Cordate, oblong-ovate

Tip: Obtuse-rounded   **Base:** Truncate-cordate   **Margin:** Entire

Inflorescence: Congested capitate or racemose cymose clusters

Florets: Corolla-funnel shaped, violet to red–purple.

Fruitlet: Globose, shiny red berry

2. *Dillenia indica*
හොඳපර, චම්පර
Up to 30m. Evergreen tree.

Leaf: Spiral Oblong

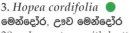

Tip: Acute/obtuse   **Base:** Rounded-acute & decurrent   **Margin:** Serrate

Flower: Sepals- yellowish green, petals-white

Fruit: Globular, yellowish green, pseudocarp

3. *Hopea cordifolia* 🟢
මෙන්දෝර, උව මෙන්දෝර
30m. Large tree with buttresses.

Leaf: Distichous Ovate-falcate

Tip: Acute-acuminate   **Base:** Cordate   **Margin:** Entire

Inflorescence: Panicle

Florets: Pale yellow

Fruit: Nut, completely enclosed in calyx, broadly spatulate, obtuse

PLATE 7

1. *Diospyros ebenum*
Ebony
කළුවර
Up to 30m. Tree. Bark-black to grey-black, rough, fissured, peeling off.

Leaf: Alternate, pellucid

Oblong-ovate-lanceolate

Tip: Obtuse-retuse

Base: Acute

Margin: Entire

Inflorescence: (male)- cyme

Florets: Male-yellow-yellowish white. Female flowers-solitary

Fruit: Depressed globose berry

2. *Diospyros montana*
Up to 14m. Tree. Live dark-yellow.

Leaf: Alternate

Subovate-oblong

Inflorescence: Male-3-flowered cyme

Tip: Acuminate

Base: Rounded/truncate/subcordate

Margin: Entire

Florets: Male- yellow/ white. Female flowers-solitary, yellow/ white

Fruit: Globose/ ovoid berry, yellow, turning to red- brown

3. *Diospyros ovalifolia*
හබර, කුණුමැල්ල
Up to 15m.Tree.

Leaf: Alternate. Lower surface- prominent midrib

Oblong oblanceolate-obovate

Tip: Obtuse/ rounded

Base: Gradually acute

Margin: Entire

Florets: Male & female corolla- yellow. Female flowers can be solitary

Fruitlet: Depressed-globose berry

1. *Maba buxifolia*
Small tree. Crown-very dense.

Leaf: Alternate

Obovate-oblong/spathulate

Tip: Obtusely acuminate, often shortly emarginated

Base: Tapering to petiole

Margin: Entire

Flower: Corolla-white, tubular

Fruit: Yellow to brown-red, ovoid to subglobose, persistent style

2. *Bridelia retusa*
කැටකැළ

5-20m. Tree. Dioecious. Young trunk-sharp spinose.

Leaf: Alternate

Elliptic-oblanceolate

Tip: Acute/obtuse/emarginate

Base: Rounded

Margin: Crenate-crisped

Inflorescence: Condensed cyme on leafless branches

Fruit: Green to yellow, globose drupe

3. *Dimorphocalyx glabellus*
වැලිවැන්න

Small trees. Moneocious.

Leaf: Alternate

Ovate-elliptic

Tip: Acute/obtuse

Base: Rounded/cuneate

Margin: Entire/crenate-undulate

Inflorescence: Short racemes (male)

Flowers: Male-large, brownish cup-shaped calyx, white petals. Female-calyx lobes-pale green, petals similar

Fruit: Globular capsule

1. *Drypetes sepiaria*
වීර
3-15m. Tree. Trunk-fluted. Bark-pale grey, flaking.

Leaf: Alternate

Elliptic (can vary)

Flower: Female flowers-1 or 2 together

Tip: Obtuse/emarginate
Base: Rounded/cordate
Margin: Entire or crenulate-serrate
Inflorescence: Male-short racemes or bracteolate clusters (male)
Fruitlet: Subglobose, bright to orange-red drupe

2. *Euphorbia antiquorum*
දළුක්
Tree. Branches-fleshy, terete or 3-several-angled. Spinous.

Leaf: Very small, fleshy

Obovate-oblong

Tip: Rounded
Base: Cuneate
Inflorescence: Short stalked cymes

Florets: Yellowish

Fruitlet: Capsule, pale brown, 3-lobed

3. *Flueggea leucopyrus*
Bushweed
හීන් කටුපිල
Bushy shrub. Twigs-terminally spinose.

Leaf: Distichous

Obovate-obcordate/rotundate

Florets: Rotate, Greenish yellow, in clusters

Tip: Retuse-emarginate
Base: Obtuse
Margin:  Entire/narrowly revolute

Fruitlet: Globose, pure white berry

PLATE 10

1. *Phyllanthus polyphyllus*
කුරටිය

2-5m. Glabrous shrub, leaves on main stem reduced to scales.

Leaflet: Oblong/Linear

Tip: Obtuse/apiculate

Base: Obtuse/rounded

Margin: Entire

Inflorescence: Condensed cyme, proximal-male florets, median-bisexual, distal-solitary female flowers

Florets: Corolla-white, rotate

Fruit: Suboblate, capsular

2. *Bauhinia racemosa*
මයිල

7m. Small tree.

Leaf: Distichous Obcordate. Conduplicate, bilobed

Tip: Lobes rounded at apex

Base: Cordate

Margin: Entire

Inflorescence: Racemose

Florets: Corolla-rotate, Yellowish-white or greenish-white

Fruit: Indehiscent, oblong, compressed black pod

3. *Bauhinia tomentosa*
කහ පෙතන්, පෙතන්

Up to 8m. Shrub or small tree.

Leaf: Distichous. Obcordate, conduplicate, bilobed

Tip: Lobes rounded at apex

Base: Cordate

Margin: Entire

Inflorescence: Racemose.

Florets: Yellow, dark purple blotch at inner petal

Fruit: Dehiscent, many-seeded pod

 A Pictorial Guide to *Uda Walawe National Park*

PLATE 11

1. *Cassia auriculata*
Matara tea
රණවරා
About 7m. Shrubs or small trees.
Leaf: Paripinnate, alternate
Leaflet: Elliptic-oblong

Tip: Mucronate/ rounded
Base: Rounded
Margin: Entire
Inflorescence: Corymbose panicle
Florets: Sepals-yellow, petals-bright yellow
Fruit: Linear oblong, compressed pod

2. *Cassia roxburghii*
Red cassia
රතු වා
10m. Tree. Umbrella shaped crown. Drooping branches.
Leaf: Paripinnate, alternate
Leaflet: Ovate-elliptic-oblong

Tip: obtuse/ retuse,
Base: Asymmetrically rounded
Margin: Entire
Inflorescence: Corymbose panicle / Panicle
Flowers: Pink or salmon
Fruit: Black, cylindrical, woody legume

3. *Crotalaria* spp.
Herbs or shrubs.
අඩන-හිරියා
Leaf: Simple, 1-foliate or digitately 3-(-7) foliolate

Inflorescence: Racemes, heads / close clusters. Can be solitary flowers

Flowers: Petals-usually yellow, sometimes white/ bluish
Fruit: Inflated dehiscent legume

1. *Derris parviflora* 🟢
කළ වැල්, සුදු කළ වැල්
Liana or scandent shrub.

Leaf: Imparipinnate, alternate

Leaflet: Ovate-oblong/obovate

Tip: Subacute/emarginate/blunt
Base: Rounded
Margin: Entire
Inflorescence: Racemose/paniculate
Florets: Calyx-reddish, petals-white/pale purplish, sweet scented
Fruit: Sessile, elliptic narrowly winged

2. *Derris scandens*
අල වැල්, බෝ කළ වැල්, කළ වැල්
About 30m. Liana.

Leaf: Imparipinnate, alternate

Oblong-obovate

Tip: Obtuse/acute/emarginate
Base: Rounded-subacute
Margin: Entire
Inflorescence: Racemose
Florets: Petals-white-pink/lavender, sweet scented
Fruit: Sessile

3. *Dichrostachys cinerea*
Bell mimosa
අන්දර
6m. Shrub or tree. Ultimate twigs-sharply spinous at the end.

Leaf: Paripinnate, distichous

Leaflet: Linear-lanceolate, unequal

Tip: Subacute
Base: Truncate
Margin: Entire
Inflorescence: Spike
Florets: Lower-violet pink, white after anthesis, upper-yellow
Fruit: Linear, indehiscent, dark brown pod

PLATE 13

1. *Pongamia pinnata*
Indian beech, Mullikulam tree
ගල් කරඳ, කරඳ, මගුල් කරඳ
About 30m. Tree, sometimes scandent.

Leaf: Imparipinnate, alternate

Leaflet: Elliptic-ovate

Tip: Acuminate
Base: Rounded
Margin: Entire-undulate
Inflorescence: Racemose

Florets: Papilionaceous. Petals-white to pinkish

Fruit: Indehiscent, obliquely oblong or elliptic pod

---

2. *Tamarindus indica* ●
Tamarind
සියඹලා, මහ සියඹලා
15-24m. Tree.

Leaf: Paripinnate

Leaflet: Oblong-elliptic

Tip: Rounded-truncate/retuse
Base: Rounded
Margin: Entire
Inflorescence: Racemose

Florets: Rotate. Calyx-reddish, petals-white/yellowish, reddish venation

Fruit: Light brown, scaly, indehiscent pod

3. *Uraria picta*
Much branched herb. Branches-densely pubescent.

Leaf: Imparipinnate, alternate

Leaflet: Narrowly oblong/lanceolate, pale central line above

Tip: Acute
Base: Rounded/subcordate
Margin: Repand
Inflorescence: Spike-like raceme

Florets: Papilionaceous. Reddish violet corolla

Fruit: Brown pod becoming pale grey

PLATE 14

1. *Alseodaphne semecarpifolia*
වැවරණි

Up to 15m. Tree, deeply fissured, yellowish brown bark.

Leaf: Spiral, crowded near tips of branchlets

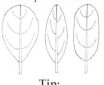

Obovate-elliptic/oblong

Tip: Obtuse/rounded/subacute
Base: Cuneate
Margin: Entire-Undulate
Inflorescence: Panicle
Florets: Salver-shaped, whitish-green
Fruit: Ellipsoid berry

2. *Hugonia mystax*
බු ගැටිය, මහ ගැටිය, වටිටි වැටි

Up to 7m. Scrambling leafy shrub.

Leaf: Alternate, crowded at ends of twigs

Oblong-oval-obovate

Tip: Obtuse
Base: Tapering
Margin: Entire-dentate
Flowers: Rotate, lower peduncles converted into spiral hooks, petals-yellow
Fruit: Globose, drupaceous, persistent sepals

3. *Strychnos nux-vomica*
Nux vomica
ගොඩ කදුරු

8-15m. Tree.

Leaf: Opposite, above-prominently 5-veined

Broadly ovate-subrotund

Tip: Obtuse, rounded, shortly acuminate
Base: Obtuse/acute, uneven
Margin: Entire
Inflorescence: Terminal cymes
Florets: Funnel-shaped, greenish
Fruit: Globose, orange to orange-red

PLATE 15

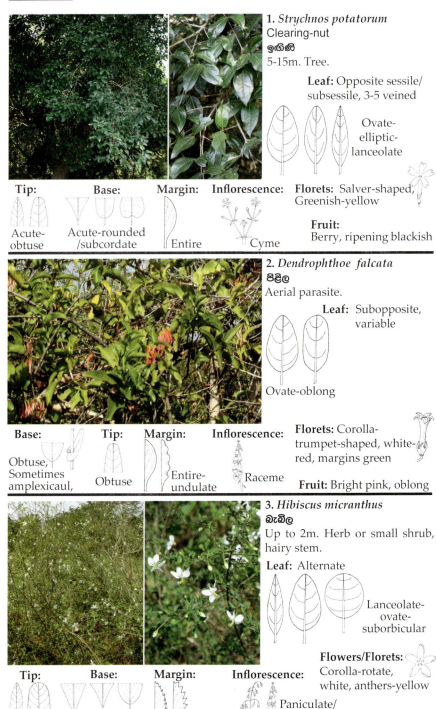

1. *Strychnos potatorum*
Clearing-nut
ඉඟිණි
5-15m. Tree.

Leaf: Opposite sessile/subsessile, 3-5 veined

Ovate-elliptic-lanceolate

Tip: Acute-obtuse
Base: Acute-rounded/subcordate
Margin: Entire
Inflorescence: Cyme
Florets: Salver-shaped, Greenish-yellow
Fruit: Berry, ripening blackish

2. *Dendrophthoe falcata*
පිළිල
Aerial parasite.

Leaf: Subopposite, variable

Ovate-oblong

Base: Obtuse, Sometimes amplexicaul,
Tip: Obtuse
Margin: Entire-undulate
Inflorescence: Raceme
Florets: Corolla-trumpet-shaped, white-red, margins green
Fruit: Bright pink, oblong

3. *Hibiscus micranthus*
බැබිල
Up to 2m. Herb or small shrub, hairy stem.

Leaf: Alternate

Lanceolate-ovate-suborbicular

Flowers/Florets: Corolla-rotate, white, anthers-yellow

Tip: Acute-rounded
Base: Cuneate-acute-obtuse
Margin: Serrate-dentate
Inflorescence: Paniculate/racemose/solitary
Fruit: Depressed-globose capsule

PLATE 16

1. *Memecylon angustifolium*
Blue mist
කොර කහ
Shrub or small tree.

Leaf: Decussate

Narrowly elliptic

Tip: Obtuse-rounded
Base: Very cuneate
Margin: Entire
Inflorescence: Thrysoid to umbel
Florets: Blue-pinkish red
Fruit: Globose, green berry

2. *Memecylon umbellatum*
Blue mist
කොර කහ
Up to 5m. Large shrub or small tree.

Leaf: Opposite
Elliptic, often channelled

Tip: Notched
Base: Cuneate
Margin: Entire
Inflorescence: Thrysoid to umbel
Florets: Petals-blue or pink, stamens-exserted
Fruit: Globose, yellowish green drupe

3. *Azadirachta indica*
Margosa Neem
කොහොඹ
Up to 16m. Tree. Bark-fissured and flaking when old.

Leaf: Imparipinnate/paripinnate
Leaflet: Falcate-lanceolate

Tip: Long acuminate
Base: Acute, asymmetric
Margin: Serrate
Inflorescence: Thyrse, paniculiform
Florets: Corolla-rotate, creamy white, styles exserted
Fruit: Ovoid-subglobose, orange-yellow drupe

A Pictorial Guide to Uda Walawe National Park

PLATE 17

1. *Walsura trifoliolata*
කිරිකෝන්, මල්පෙත්ත
Tree.

Leaf: Alternate, trifoliolate

Leaflet: Oblong-oval

Tip:	Base:	Margin:	Inflorescence:
Obtuse	Acute	Entire	Dense panicle

Florets:
Corolla rotate
White/pinkish

Fruit: Ovoid, hairy, orange-brown berry

2. *Ficus benghalensis*
Banyan
මහ නුග
Large banyan. Aerial roots. present

Leaf: Spiral

Ovate

Tip:	Base:	Margin:	Inflorescence:
Obtuse	Cordate	Entire	Hypanthodium (a cross section)

Inflorescence fruit (fig): Sessile, ripening orange to red, depressed-globose, separate female and male flowers

---

3. *Streblus asper*
Crooked rough-bush
ගැට නෙටුල්
Bush or small tree. Drooping branches.

Leaf: Alternate

Elliptic-obovate

Tip:	Base:	Margin:
Acute, mucronate	Attenuate (vary), slightly asymmetric	Serrate (vary)

Florets:
(male)-Fragrant, white stamens.
Female flowers-solitary, green

Fruit: Yellow-orange drupe, globose or 2-humped at base

PLATE 18

1. *Streblus taxoides*
Fig-lime
ගොන් ගොටු
Small twiggy tree. Woody spinous.

Leaf: Distichous

Elliptic, ovate-obovate, asymmetric

Tip:	Base:	Margin:	Inflorescence: head (male). Solitary female flowers
Acute-long acuminate, tridentate	Cuneate-slightly rounded	Dentate, spiny	**Florets:** Greenish **Fruit:** Ellipsoid, asymmetric drupe covered by enlarged tepals

2. *Eucalyptus* spp. ●
Trees. Twisted, unbuttressed. Bark-exfoliating.

Leaf: Pendent, young-red, aromatic, pellucid-punctate, opposite, rotundate, varying from intermediate to mature stage

Inflorescence:

Umbel or   Panicle

Fruit: Dry capsule

3. *Eugenia bracteata*
තැඹිලිය
Much-branched shrub / small tree. Many organs pubescent.

Leaf: Opposite, intermarginal veins.
Elliptic

Tip: Retuse/subacuminate

Base:	Margin:	Inflorescence:	Florets:
Cuneate, obtuse	Entire	Reduced cyme	Corolla-rotate, cream

Fruit: Pyriform-subglobose, green-yellow-red, persistent sepals

A Pictorial Guide to *Uda Walawe National Park*

PLATE 19

1. *Syzygium cumini*
මා දං, මහ දං
Large shrub to canopy tree.

Leaf: Decussate, Intermarginal nerve straight

Elliptic-ovate-lanceolate

Tip: Acumen, subequal
Base: Cuneate, shortly decurrent
Margin: Undulate
Inflorescence: Cyme

Florets: Petals- whitish, opening-very small, stamens-many

Fruit: Broadly ellipsoid berry, ripening purple

2. *Ochna lanceolata*
බෝ කෑර, මල් කෑර
3m. Shrubs or treelets.

Leaf: Distichous

Ovate/elliptic-lanceolate

Tip: Rounded-acute
Base: Acute-rounded
Margin: Crenately denticulate
Inflorescence: Raceme/ solitary flowers

Florets: Corolla - bright yellow.

Fruit: Drupelet, persistent sepals enlarged in fruit. Greenish, becomes black

3. *Jasminum auriculatum*
Scandent shrub or vine.

Leaf: Unifoliolate / trifoliolate, opposite

Elliptic-ovate

Tip: Rounded-acute
Base: Rounded
Margin: Entire
Inflorescence: Cymose paniculate, subcorymbose

Florets: Corolla- Salver-shaped, white.

Fruit: Paired berry / often single, ellipsoid-spheroid, ripened-purple-black

1. *Panicum maximum* ●
Guinea grass
රට තණ
1-3m. Tufted perennial often forming large clumps.

Leaf: Blades-wide, linear, flat

Linear

Tip: Tapering **Base:** Often narrowed at base **Inflorescence:** Panicle **Florets:** Spikelets-green or flushed with purple, stigmas-purple

Fruit: Caryopsis

2. *Scutia myrtina*
2-5m. Straggling or scandent shrub, rarely small trees.

Leaf: Decussate.

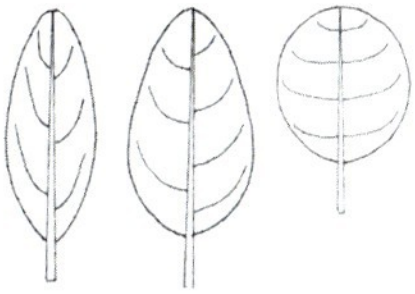

Elliptic-ovate/orbicular

Tip: Acute-obtuse/retuse-emarginated always mucronulate **Base:** Rounded to cuneate **Margin:** Entire **Inflorescence:** Condensed cyme **Florets:** Salver-shaped, pale-white or yellowish green

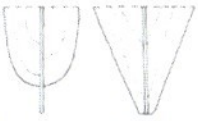

Fruit: Drupe, young-pale, mature-purplish or bluish-black

3. *Ventilago madraspatana*
යකා වැල්, යකඩ වැල්
Much branched woody climber.

Leaf: Alternate

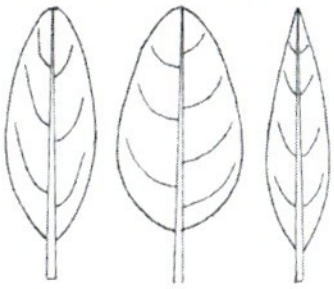

Elliptic-ovate-lanceolate

Tip: Acute or subacuminate **Base:** Rounded/slightly oblique **Margin:** Entire or crenate **Inflorescence:** Panicle **Florets:** Yellowish-green, 5 petals

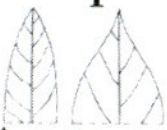

Fruit: Samaroid globose nut with a wing

PLATE 21

1. *Ziziphus oenoplia*
හීන් එරමිණියා
3-5m. Stragling or climbing shrubs. Branchlets-hairy, spiny.

Leaf: Alternate

Obliquely ovate-lanceolate

Tip: Acute-acuminate
Base: Obliquely subacute
Margin: Minutely denticulate
Inflorescence: Cyme
Florets: Corolla-rotate, green
Fruit: Globose or ovoid drupe, shinning and black when ripe

2. *Benkara malabarica*
පුදන්
Shrub armed with short spines.

Leaf: Elliptic-obovate/oblanceolate

Tip: Obtuse, slightly apiculate
Base: Cuneate
Margin: Entire
Florets: Corolla-salver-shaped, white
Fruit: Globose berry, ripening red

3. *Canthium coromandelicum*
කර
Up to 5m. Much branched shrub, spinous.

Leaf: Ovate-elliptic/obovate

Tip: Acute-acuminate
Base: Acute-obtuse
Margin: Entire
Inflorescence: Axillary cymes from short shoots
Florets: Greenish, stamens-exserted
Fruit: Suborbicular drupe

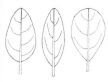

PLATE 22

1. *Catunaregam spinosa*
කුකුර්මාන්, කුකුරුමාන්
Shrub or small tree with small straight spines.

Leaf: Obovate-almost round

Tip: Obtuse   Base: Attenuate   Margin: Entire

Flowers: salver-shaped White when young, turning to cream, stamens, styles-exserted, two large round stigmas

Fruit: Berry

2. *Haldina cordifolia*
කොලොන්
7-30m. Deciduous tree. Bole-buttressed, bark-reddish brown.

Leaf: Broadly ovate

Tip: Slightly acute   Base: Cordate   Margin: Entire   Inflorescence: Head

Florets: Yellowish, corolla-outside densely hairy

3. *Mitragyna parviflolia*
හැළඹ
30m. Large deciduous tree.

Leaf: Elliptic-obovate (variable)

Tip: Rounded-acute   Base: Obtuse-subcordate   Margin: Entire   Inflorescence: Head

Florets: White

Fruit: Capsule

A Pictorial Guide to Uda Walawe National Park

PLATE 23

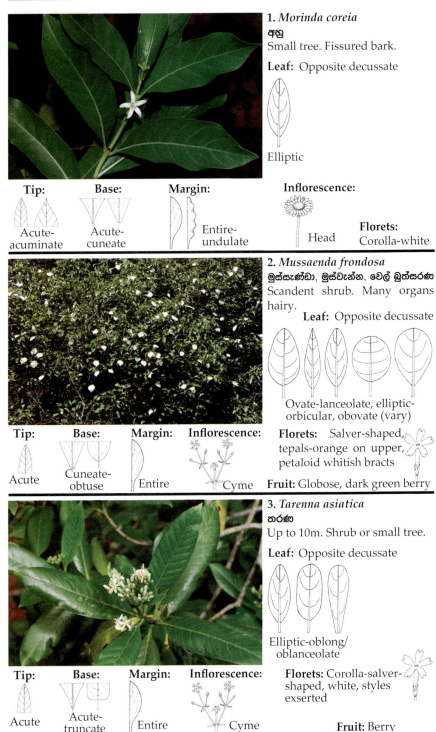

1. *Morinda coreia*
අහු
Small tree. Fissured bark.

Leaf: Opposite decussate

Elliptic

Tip: Acute-acuminate
Base: Acute-cuneate
Margin: Entire-undulate
Inflorescence: Head
Florets: Corolla-white

2. *Mussaenda frondosa*
මුස්සැණ්ඩා, මුස්වැන්න, වෙල් බුත්සරණ
Scandent shrub. Many organs hairy.

Leaf: Opposite decussate

Ovate-lanceolate, elliptic-orbicular, obovate (vary)

Tip: Acute
Base: Cuneate-obtuse
Margin: Entire
Inflorescence: Cyme
Florets: Salver-shaped, tepals-orange on upper, petaloid whitish bracts
Fruit: Globose, dark green berry

3. *Tarenna asiatica*
තරණ
Up to 10m. Shrub or small tree.

Leaf: Opposite decussate

Elliptic-oblong/oblanceolate

Tip: Acute
Base: Acute-truncate
Margin: Entire
Inflorescence: Cyme
Florets: Corolla-salver-shaped, white, styles exserted
Fruit: Berry

PLATE 24

1. *Atalantia monophylla*
Small tree with spines.

Leaf: Alternate

 Ovate/elliptic

Tip: Obtuse, clearly notched

Base: Cuneate

Margin: Entire-undulate

Inflorescence: Racemose, fascicled

Florets: Corolla-white.

Fruit: Globose, yellowish green hesperidium

2. *Chloroxylon swietenia*
Satinwood

Deciduous tree. Most organs pubescent.

Leaf: Alternate, paripinnate

Leaflet: Oblong, semi-cordate

Tip: Obtuse-acute

Base: Obtuse, asymmetric

Margin: Entire

Inflorescence: Raceme

Florets: Corolla-white

Fruit: Oblong-ovoid capsule

3. *Glycosmis mauritiana*
Up to 3m. Shrub. Finely cracked bark.

Leaf: Tri-pentafoliate, alternate

Leaflets: Elliptic-ovate/obovate

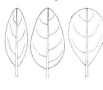

Tip: Acuminate-subacute

Base: Acuminate/obtuse

Margin: Entire

Inflorescence: Short panicle

Florets: Corolla-white.

Fruit: Subglobose, pink / salmon berry

A Pictorial Guide to Uda Walawe National Park

1. *Limonia acidissima*
Elephant-apple, Woodapple
දිවුල්

Up to 7m. Small tree. Spiny branchlets.

Leaf: Alternate, imparipinnate

Leaflet: Obovate, laterals-sessile

Tip: Obtuse/retuse
Base: Acute-obtuse
Margin: Entire
Inflorescence: Cymose-paniculate

Flowers: Corolla-rotate, white green / reddish-purplish

Fruit: woody, globose berry, pale ashy-brownish

2. *Murraya paniculata*
Orange jessamine
ඇටිටේරියා

Shrub or small tree.

Leaf: Alternate, imparipinnate

Leaflet: Ovate-elliptic

Tip: Acuminate
Base: Cuneate-rounded
Margin: Entire / Crenate
Inflorescence: Paniculate

Florets: Corolla-salver-shaped, petals-5, white

Fruit: Ovoid, pointed berry

3. *Paramignya monophylla*
වෙල්ලන්ගිරිය

Woody climber. Densely pubescent young shoots. Old branches spiny.

Leaf: Alternate

Oblong-ovate/lanceolate

Tip: Obtuse-acute/emarginate
Base: Rounded
Margin: Entire
Inflorescence: Cyme / fascicle

Florets: Petals-white.

Fruit: Globose-obovoid pyriform, angular or furrowed berry, pubescent

PLATE 26

1. *Pleiospermium alatum*
තුම්පත් කුරුඳු, තුන්පත් කුරුඳු
Small tree.

Leaf: Trifoliolate, alternate. Winged petiole
Leaflet: Obovate-oblanceolate

Tip: Rounded-emarginate
Base: Cuneate
Margin: Entire
Inflorescence: Panicle
Florets: Petals-white
Fruit: Globose berry, like a small orange

2. *Lepisanthes tetraphylla*
Shrub or moderate sized tree.

Leaf: Paripinnate, alternate
Leaflet: Elliptic-oblong-lanceolate

Tip: Obtuse-rounded/acuminate
Base: Acute/rounded
Margin: Entire
Inflorescence: Panicle
Florets: White-reddish, Male-4 petals, female-4/5
Fruit: Oblong-ovoid drupe, densely hairy, yellow

3. *Sapindus emarginata*
Soap nut tree
පෙනෙල, කහ පෙනෙල
Medium-large sized tree, much branched spreading crown.

Leaf: Paripinnate, alternate
Leaflet: Oblanceolate/elliptic-ovate

Tip: Emarginate-retuse
Base: Acute-cuneate
Margin: Entire
Inflorescence: Panicle
Florets: Petals-white
Fruit: Rusty-brown berry

A Pictorial Guide to Uda Walawe National Park

PLATE 27

1. *Schleichera oleosa*
Ceylon oak
කෝන්
Tree.

Leaf: Paripinnate, alternate

Leaflet: Oblong

Tip:	Base:	Margin:	Inflorescence:
Rounded	Attenuate, teparing	Undulate	Panicle

Florets: Green

Fruit: Ovoid, sharply pointed, green drupe.

2. *Manilkara hexandra*
පලු
3-20m. Shrub / tree with spreading crown. Bark-deeply longitudinally fissured.

Leaf: Spiral

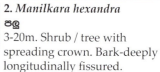 Oblong-obovate/elliptic

Tip:	Base:	Margin:	Inflorescence:
Rounded/emarginate	Cuneate	Entire, revolute	Fascicle

Florets: Corolla-white

Fruit: Yellowish/orange, ellipsoid berry

3. *Grewia damine*
දමිණිය
Up to 10m. Large shrub to small tree.

Leaf: Alternate

Obovate/ovate

Tip:	Base:	Margin:	Inflorescence:
Rounded-emarginate	Cordate-truncate-rounded	Crenate-serrate	Umbel

Florets: Yellow

Fruit: Depressed-globose drupe, dry-black

PLATE 28

1. *Grewia orientalis*
වැල් කෙළිය, වැල් මැදිය
3-4m. Shrub.

Leaf: Alternate

Ovate-elliptic

Tip: Acute-subobtuse/acuminate
Base: Subcordate-obtuse
Margin: Crenulate
Inflorescence: Umbel
Florets: White
Fruit: depressed-globose gonophore, black with brown dots when dry

2. *Holoptelea integrifolia*
Indian Elm
ගොඩ කිරිල්ල
Deciduous tree. Bark-offensive smell.

Leaf: Distichous

Elliptic

Tip: Acute-acuminate
Base: Obtuse-subcordate
Margin: Entire
Inflorescence: Or fascicle (male bisexual mixed) Short raceme
Florets: Greenish yellow-brownish Perianth-4
Fruit: Winged, compressed samara

3. *Gmelina asiatica*
Asiatic beechberry
දෙමට, ගැට දෙමට
Large bush / shrub / tree / prostrate. Spiny or not.

Leaf:

Ovate-elliptic/obovate (vary)

Tip: Acute-abtuse
Base: Acute-cuneate/rounded
Margin: Entire
Inflorescence: Racemiform panicle
Florets: Corolla-large, yellow / bright sulphur yellow, bilabiate
Fruit: Ovoid or obovoid-pyriform drupe, ripe-yellow

A Pictorial Guide to

PLATE 29

1. *Lantana camara* ●

ගඳපාන, ගර්ඳපාන, ගෙඳපාන, කටු හිඟුරු, ටොන්කිකුද්ඳු

Shrub.

Leaf: Decussate

Ovate

Tip: Acute/acuminate

Base: Acutely narrowed

Margin: Crenate-serrate

Inflorescence: Head

Florets: Corolla-salver shaped, mostly opening yellow, pink in age or orange to red or scarlet

Fruit: Purple or black drupe

2. *Premna tomentosa*

බූ සයිරු ගස්, බූ සේරු, නූ සයිරු

Shrub/tree. Branches-tetragonal, hairy.

Leaf: Decussate

Ovate-oblong

Tip: Acute/caudate

Base: Acute/rounded

Margin: Entire

Inflorescence: Cyme

Flowers: Corolla-white/greenish to yellow, slightly bilabiate.

Fruit: drupaceous, subglobose, green to purple to black (ripen)

3. *Tectona grandis* ●

Indian oak, Teak

තේක්ක

Large tree. Branches-tetragonal.

Leaf: Decussate

Elliptic

Inflorescence: Panicle and cyme

Flowers: Corolla-salver shaped, white/pinkish

Fruit: Drupaceous, subglobose/flattened, brown hairs

Tip: Acute, acuminate

Base: Acute, acuminate, clasping

Margin: Entire/repand denticulate

PLATE 30

1. *Vitex altissima*
මිල්ල
Large tree. Drooping.

Leaf: Opposite-decussate, trifoliolate

Leaflet: Subequal, Central leaflet- elliptic

Tip: Caudate/acuminate

Base: Acuminate/shortly attenuate

Margin: Entire

Inflorescence: Paniculate

Florets: Corolla-salver shaped, light pink/white and bluish to purple, bilabiate

Fruit: Drupaceous, spheroidal, green-blackish, white dots

2. *Vitex negundo*
Chaste Tree
හෙළරික, නික, නිල් නික, සුදු නික, නිර්ගුණ්ඩි
Large shrub/small deciduous tree.

Leaf: Opposite decussate, Trifoliolate.

Leaflet: Oblong/elliptic/lanceolate

Tip: Attenuate or subacuminate

Base: Acute/acuminate

Margin: Entire-serrate/dentate

Inflorescence: Panicle

Florets: Blue-lavender, pink/white, corolla-salver shaped, bilabiate

3. *Cissus quadrangularis*
හිරැස්ස, සීරැස්ස
Succulent, deciduous liane. Apical stems-quadrangular, green.

Leaf: Ovate-deltoid

Tip: Obtuse

Base: Truncate

Inflorescence: Cyme

Flowers: Petals-pale green.

Fruit: Subglobose berry, maroon. Persistent calyx and style

Plate 31

1. *Cissus vitiginea*
වල් නිවිති
Deciduous liane with unpleasant smell. Tendrils present.

Leaf: Alternate, palmately 5-lobed

Ovate or rounded (variable)

Florets: Petals-pale yellow-green

Fruit: Ovoid to obovoid, pendulous berry, purple-blue-black with glaucous 'bloom'

Tip: Acute/obtuse
Base: Truncate-cordate
Margin: Irregularly Dentate
Inflorescence: False umbel

2. *Pterospermum suberifolium*
Fishing rod tree
වෙලන්, වෙලන්ගු, වෙලුන්
Shrub or tree. Fluted bole and fissured bark.

Leaf: Distichous

Oblong/obovate

Inflorescence: Cyme

Florets: Petals-yellow or white

Fruit: Ellipsoid capsule, densely whitish or rusty tomentose

Tip: Acute- acuminate/rounded
Base: Oblique and Subcordate-truncate
Margin: Entire/irregularly undulate

---

3. *Clausena indica*
මී ගොන් කරපිංචා
Up to 5m. Shrub or small tree.

Leaf: Imparipinnate, alternate

Leaflet: Ovate-lanceolate

Florets: petals-greenish or white

Fruit: subglobose berry, cream to salmon colour

Tip: Acuminate
Base: Asymmetric
Margin: Subentire/minutely subcrenulate
Inflorescence: Paniculate

PLATE 32

1. *Stereospermum colais*
ලුණු මඩල, දුනු මඩල
Up to 25m. Large tree.

Leaf: Imparipinnate

Leaflet: Elliptic-oblong

Tip: Caudate **Base:** Acute **Margin:**  Entire **Inflorescence:** Paniculate **Florets:** Corolla-dull pink to yellow **Fruit:** Capsule

---

2. *Acacia leucophloea*
කටු අන්දර, මහ අන්දර
Up to 10m. Tree.

Leaf: Compound, bipinnate

Leaflet: Sessile
Oblong-linear

Tip: Rounded-mucronulate **Base:** Truncate **Margin:** Entire **Inflorescence:** Panicle **Florets:** White **Fruit:** Legume, strap-shaped, fleshy

---

3. *Capparis zeylanica*
සුදු වෙලන්ගිරිය
0.75-1m. Erect or straggling much branched shrub, thorns present.

Leaf: Ovate-elliptic-lanceolate

Tip: Acute- rounded/ obtuse **Base:** Rounded-subcordate **Margin:** Entire **Flower:** Solitary or paired axillary, white, upper pair of petals yellow at base, become reddish violet with age

Fruit: Berry, ripening red, orange or purple.

PLATE 33

1. *Erythroxylum zeylanicum*
3m. Much branched shrubs.

Leaf: Alternate

Lanceolate, elliptic

Tip: Acute/acuminate
Base: Truncate
Margin: Entire

Flowers: Axillary, yellowish green

Fruit: Drupe, ovoid-oblong, deep red when ripe, persistent calyx.

2. *Toddalia asiatica*
කුඩු-මිරිස්
Small climber.

Leaf: Alternate, trifoliolate with sessile leaflets.

Leaflet: Ovate to oblong-lanceolate

Tip: Bluntly acuminate
Base: Acute
Margin: Shallowly crenulate
Inflorescence: Paniculate
Florets: Unisexual

Fruit: subglobose drupe, orange when ripe

3. *Mallotus rhamnifolius*
Shrub or small tree, 1.5—8 m.

Leaf: Opposite towards ends of branches.

Lanceolate to ovate-lanceolate

Tip: Acute to long acuminate, obtuse
Base: Narrowed or rounded
Margin: Entire to minutely denticulate

Flowers: Separate male and female inflorescences.

Fruit: Densely pubescent.

A Pictorial Guide to National Park

1. *Miliusa indica*
කැකිලි-මැස්ස
Densely branched tree or treelet.

Leaf: Ovate / elliptic

Tip: Obtuse/ acute

Base:  Rounded/ truncate/ subcordate

Margin: Entire

Flower: Sloitary, yellow and purple

Fruitlets: Ovoid, purple

2. *Salacia reticulata*
කොතල හිඹුටු, හිඹුටු වැල්
Woody climber or scandent shrub.

Leaf: Opposite

Elliptic/ oval

Tip:

Obtuse/

Base: Acute

Margin: Entire/ crenate-serrate

Flowers: In inflorescences.

Florets: Greenish yellow.

Fruit: Globose, drupaceous, bright pink-orange when ripe.

3. *Eupatorium odoratum*
1-2.5m. Erect or sprawling shrub.

Leaf: Opposite

Deltoid-ovate

Tip: Acuminate attenuate,

Base: Cuneate

Margin: Dentate

Inflorescence: 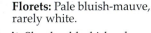 Capitulum

Florets: Pale bluish-mauve, rarely white.

Fruit: Slender, blackish achene, pappus whitish or pale brown when dried

Molluscs

(Plate 35-36)

Molluscs, typically snails, slugs, mussels, etc., are one of the most important faunal groups found in Sri Lanka. Home in water and on land, most of them have a shell. Some have two shells and they are called 'bivalves' while most have a single shell. Both types belong to the group Gastropoda. There are also a few which do not have a shell, called slugs, and these are found on land. They feed mainly on vegetables by rasping, for which they have a radula which is a row of teeth, constantly renewed, located on the floor of the mouth. They move by gliding over a mucous layer secreted by the 'foot'. Many of the Molluscs in Sri Lanka are endemic to the island.

MOLLUSCS

These scavengers are hardy and often survive drought by encasing themselves in mud. Molluscs move about by clinging to vegetation or by travelling on the ground although at times they are seen moving about on the surface of water with the body hanging downwards.

Operculate Gastropods
These molluscs have a horny operculum attached to the foot; this covers the cavity. During times of drought molluscs survive by encasing themselves in a sealed shell.

1. *Paludomus zeylanica*
2. *Bithynia inconspicus*
3. *Pila globosa*
4. *Bellamya ceylonica*
5. *Melanoides tuberculata*
6. *Indoplanorbis exustus*
7. *Lymnaea pinguis*

Bivalve Molluscs
Bivalves have two shells or 'valves'. They are generally observed buried in muddy or sandy bottoms. Feeding is through a filter system.

8. *Lamellidens marginalis*

PLATE 36

LAND SNAILS

Sri Lanka has a rich land snail fauna of around 300 species. More than 80% of them are endemic. They belong to two major groups – the prosobranchs, with a pair of tentacles bearing the eyes at the tip, and the pulmonates, with a pair of tentacles without eyes (which are placed at the base of the tentacles). They also have a hard "operculum" that closes the opening when the body is taken into the shell.

1. *Beddomea trifasciatus* (Lowland form) ●
   5mm. Pulmonate. Robust shell with spots and stripes.

2. *Euplecta* spp. ●
   5mm. Pulmonate. Thin fragile shell, heavily marked with spots and stripes.

3. *Rhachistia pulcher*
   5mm. Pulmonate. A clear central line in the middle of the whorls. Arboreal.

4. *Mirus panos* ●
   3mm. Pulmonate. Elongated shell. The lips are flattened. Arboreal.

5. *Eurychlamys vilipensa*
   3mm. Pulmonate. Thin fragile shell. Plain.

6. *Cryptozona bistrialis*
   10mm. Prosobranch. Bulbulous shell, with sharp edged lips. Colour changes with age from orange–red in juveniles to blackish–grey in adults.

7. *Aulopoma itieri* var. *hofmeisteri* ●
   10mm. Prosobranch. The thick operculum fits the shell aperture like a lid. Found among the ground leaf litter.

8. *Pterocyclus troscheli* ●
   10mm. Prosobranch. Operculum surface on the outside ornamented with ridges. Found among the ground leaf litter. Veriagated colours.

9. *Theobaldius* spp. ●
   5mm. Prosobranch. Thick operculum fits over the shell aperture like a lid. Found among the ground leaf litter.

10. *Micraulax coeloconus*
    5mm. Prosobranch. Found on the ground among leaf litter.

Arthropoda

(Plates 37-41)

The arthropods are a very widespread group of animals and comprise 75% of all species described to date. The common feature is that their limbs are segmented, like the body. The body often consist of a head, thorax, and abdomen. The appendages in the body are modified to perform different functions. In the head they are modified for feeding, while in the thorax and abdomen they are modified mostly for movement. This diverse group has a chitinous body cover in most cases. Based on the number of limbs they are generally divided into Class Insecta with six legs and Class Arachnida with eight. Class Crustacea of Phylum Arthropoda are mostly inhabitants of water although some crustaceans have invaded land.

PLATE 37

AQUATIC ARTHROPODS

These "joint-limbed" organisms are adapted to living in water. They occupy different niches within the water column.

Water Bugs
Insect with an interesting habit: the female lays its eggs on the body of the male and the male carries the eggs until they hatch.
   1. *Lethocerus indicus*
       A big and powerful carnivore, it can reach to 3 inches in size. Brown colour
   2. *Sphaeroderma rusticum*
       Brown colour. Often found among water weeds.

Whirlygig Beetles
Surface swimmers and gregarious, these beetles are found constantly darting around in circles, hence the name. When disturbed they quickly dive underwater.
   3. *Gyrinus* spp.

Back Swimmers / Boatman
These insects are inhabitants of open waters, swim upside down but are capable of flight.
   4. *Anisops barbata*

Diving Beetles
These beetles swim in the water often coming up for air. The air is tucked under the elytra of the wing
   5. *Cybister* spp.

Digging Beetles
Fast swimming beetles found under the substratum along the bottom and edges.
   6. *Hydrocoptus* spp.

Water Scorpion
A carnivorous species seen among water weeds, it has a long back tube for breathing air.
   7. *Laccotrephes grossus*

Water Striders
These insects swim about on the surface of the water and are often found in clustering in the shade.
   8. *Gerris adelaidis*

Water Stick Insect
Another carnivore also observed among water weeds, this insect has a long back tube for breathing air.
   9. *Ranatra filiformis*

Fresh water Lobster
Large lobsters characteristic with large claws. Under rocks among leaf litter
   10. *Macrobrachium rosenbergii*

Fresh water Crab
An extensive group, almost 99% endemic.
   11. *Parathelpheus* spp; *Ceylonothalpheus* spp., etc.

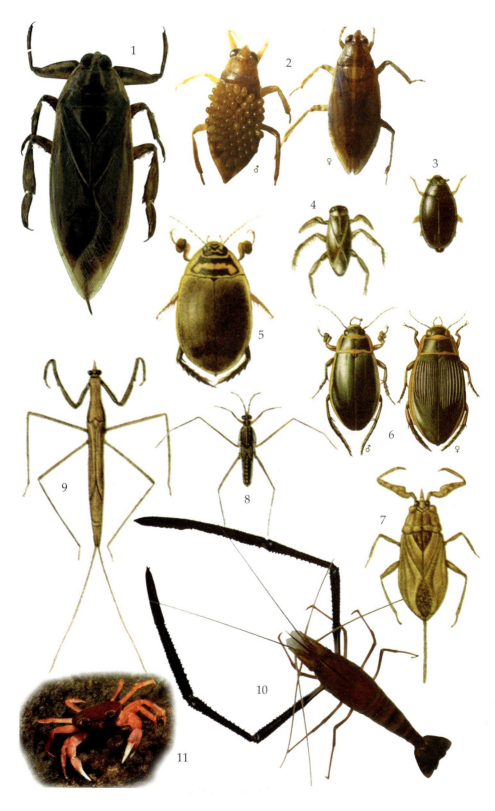

PLATE 38

INSECT LARVAE

1. *Trichoptera* (Caddisfly) Larvae
   Found at bottom of waterholes amongst vegetation.

2. *Anophiline* (Mosquito) Larvae
   Inhabits water surface.

3. *Neuroptera* (Alderfly) Larvae
   Lives among vegetation.

4. *Odonata* (Damselfly) Larvae
   Found in vegetationat the water's edge.

5. *Odonata* (Dragonfly) Larvae
   Inhabits edges of bodies of water.

6. *Cybister* (Water Beetle) Larvae
   Bottom dwellers in shallow water.

7. *Odonata* (Mayfly) Larvae
   Found amongst vegetation.

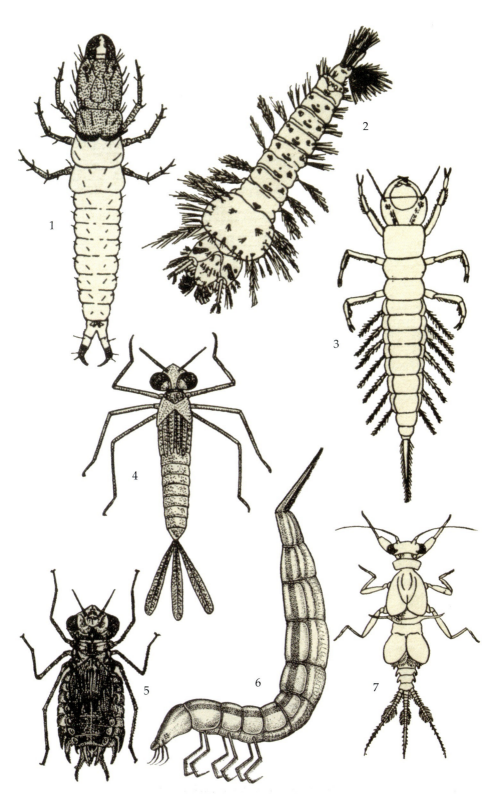

TERSTRIAL ARTHROPODS - I

1. Grasshoppers *Tethigonia* spp.
   Often green colour with opaque wings. Females posses large oviposters at the back. Long antennae> strong large "saltatory" back legs.

2. *Dysdercus ungulates*
   Often seen in mating position. In small groups among leaf litter.

3. Fire Flies *Luciola* spp.
   Active in the night, the flickering lights seperate the species.

4. Praying Mantis *Mantis* spp.
   Females are generally bigger. Carnivorous. Capture the prey with front limbs. Comes in diverse colours. And shapes.

5. Cricket *Acheta* spp.
   Makes high pitch sounds in the evenings and night. The call is the mating call. Often made by stridulating the wings or hind legs.

6. Cicarda *Tibicen* spp.
   About 12 species in Sri Lanka. The high pitch screeth made as the day picks up from among the foliage. These adult flies emerge from the long larval life in the soil to mate and die. Feeds on plant sap.

7. Lady bird Beetles *Coccinella* spp.
   A very diverse group of colourful small beetles. Vegetarian

8. Earwig *Forficula* spp.
   The two pincers at the back are characteristic. Found among detritus and in banana combs, etc.

9. Coackoroach *Blatta* spp.
   Smaller than domestic variety and sometimes black. Often seen scurrying for cover among leaf litter.

10. Mole Ant *Gyroptalpa* spp.
    The forelimb is modified to dig into the ground like a mole. Nocturnal, usually seen running after prey. During daytime it stays underground.

PLATE 40

TERRSTRIAL ARTHROPODS - II

1. Centipedes *Scolopander* spp.
   Body segment rectangular with one pair of legs. Strong jaws in the front.

2. Millipedes
   Segmented body with two pairs of legs. Flat or rounded body.
   - 2-i. *Julis* spp. - Small-sized, flat, black with yellow lines on sides.
   - 2-ii. Millipede - Medium-sized, rounded. Body colour red with lighter coloured legs.
   - 2-iii. Millipede - Large-sized, rounded. Body colour black with lighter coloured legs.

3. Ant Fly (Ant Lion) *Distoleon tetragrammicus*
   Larvae make cone like depressions in the sand and lie in wait at the bottom for prey to tumble in. Adult with delicate opaque wings.

4. Fire Fly *Luciola* spp.
   Female:- Medium-sized, flat head. Phosphorescent light at vent.

5. Cattle Ticks *Rhipicephalus microplus*
   Found attached to the body of cattle, occasional on dogs. When gorged with blood appears grey-black.

6. Scoprion *Heterometrus swarmmerdami*
   Small to large. Sting at the last node of the body. It strikes with the tail curving over body as it holds the prey with front pincers.

BEES, WASPS & HORNETS

1. Honey Bee *Apis cerena*
   මීමැස්සා
   The common honey bees that make honey. In the wild they form colonies in tree cavities and under rocks.

2. Rock Honey Bee *Apis dorsata*
   බම්බරා
   Their dark hives are seen suspended on high branches and in rock cavities. The honey is strongly flavoured.

3. Dwarf Honey Bee *Apis florae*
   දඬුවැල් මීමැස්සා
   Colonies of this species form hives on small branches and move often. Thus the Sinhala name.

4. Stingless Honey Bee *Trigona iridipennis*
   කණේයියා
   Common in small tree holes and in rock crevices. The outer mouth of the colony has a distinctive blackish exudate. Contains little honey but with medicinal value.

5. Gaint Carpenter Bee *Xylocopa tenuiscapa*
   අම්බලන් පාළුවා
   Bores holes in wooden rafters of buildings and dry twigs in the forest. Visits flowers in the vicinity of these holes.

6. Hornet *Vespa orientalis*
   දෙබරා
   Unmistakable black and orangeish yellow. Stings can be dangerous and colonies can attack in a swarm. The nest is made of a wood pulp and mud mix.

7. Potter wasp *Eumenes coarctatus*
   කුඹලා
   Generally unaggressive. Makes 'pots' suspended on branches to place eggs, along with food for larvae. Prey is usually transported partially anaesthetized. Shapes of 'pots' can vary with species.

Dung beetles
(Plate 42)

Dung beetles (Coleoptera: Scarabaeinae) perform key roles in tropical forests. They have roles in waste removal, secondary seed dispersal, and parasite suppression. Dung beetles are divided into three functional groups; rollers, tunnelers, and dwellers. Their front legs are specially modified to form a ball with dung and this sphere is rolled into an underground chamber to feed larvae.

Plate 42

1. ***Paragymnopleurus koenegi***
   11.5mm. **Roller.** Shiny black body with yellowish-white blotches. Often seen in large numbers on human faecal matter.

2. ***Copris signatus***
   15mm. **Tunneller.** Flat brownish black body. Usually attracted to cow dung.

3. ***Catharsius molossus***
   30mm. **Tunneller.** Widespread and abundant.

4. ***Copris sodalis***
   14.5mm. **Tunneller.** Shiny blackish brown. The head bears a slender erect horn or a slight transverse elevation.

5. ***Onthophagus gazella***
   13mm. **Tunneller.** Greenish brown body. Prominent pair of slender horns.

6. ***Onthophagus difficilis***
   5.5mm. **Tunneler.** Prominent black-striated brown body.

7. ***Onthophagus militaris***
   6mm. **Tunneler.** Black body with prominent yellow orange spots. Characteristic hairy appearance.

8. ***Onthophagus spinifex***
   10mm. **Tunneller.** Variable colour: black, metallic blue, greenish black, purplish black, etc. Long and short horned morphs but sometimes hornless.

9. ***Onthophagus unifasciatus***
   6mm. **Tunneler.** Brown body with large yellow patches. Associated with scarabiasis illness ('Kurumini maandama' in Sinhalese).

10. ***Paragymnopleurus melanarius***
    18mm. **Roller.** Flat compact body with long legs give this beetle a spidery form. Heavily affected by the loss of forest cover.

Spiders

(Plates 43-45)

Spiders evoke fear in many and are often misunderstood. Their webs are wonders of natural architecture. They can be easily distinguished from other insects because they have two body segments: the cephalothorax and the abdomen. Spiders possess up to eight simple eyes and four pair of legs. Spinnerets (silk weaving structures) are on the posterior end. There are around 501 known species of spiders in Sri Lanka, with probably another thousand waiting to be discovered.

Female spiders are generally larger than males. Using sight, vibration, and touch they target insects and other prey alighting or walking nearby. Some prey may be bigger than the spider. The best known method of prey capture is by means of sticky webs. Spiders immobilize their prey in two ways - by biting and injecting paralyzing venom, and by silk swathing and wrapping.

Spiders avoid human beings and bite only in self-defense. Even so, only a handful produce venom that cause a reaction.

PLATE 43

1. **Sri Lanka Pedersen's Tiger Spider** *Poecilotheria pederseni* ●
   ශ්‍රී ලංකා පෙඩර්සර්න්ගේ දිවි මකුළුවා
   5-8cm. Arboreal. Nocturnal. Triangular dark patch on ventral side of the fourth leg.

2. **Ornate Tree trunk Spider** *Herennia multipuncta*
   ආසියා විසිතුරු පැතලි මකුළුවා
   5-8cm. Arboreal. Male spider is small, red in colour, and lives with the female.

3. **Brown Sailor Spider** *Neoscona nautica*
   පොදු ගෙවතු මකුළුවා
   1.8cm. Nocturnal. Common in open areas. Body colour black and brown. There is a cross mark on the abdomen.

4. **Common Kite Spider / Common Spiny-orb Weaver** *Gasteracantha geminata*
   පොදු සරුංගල් මකුළුවා
   0.7cm. Body colour black, yellow, and white. Two spiny protrusions at the dorsal surface of abdomen. Constructs an orb web.

5. **Signature Spider** *Argiope anasuja*
   ලියන දැල් වියන්නා
   1.2cm. Very common. Black, yellow, and white colour pattern. Orb-shaped web.

6. **Giant Wood Spider** *Nephila pilipes*
   යෝධ වන මකුළුවා
   6-7cm. Head ashy white and abdomen black and yellow. Inhibits riverine forest in the Dry Zone. An orb web weaver. Male is tiny and red in colour.

7. **Common Long-jawed Orbweaver** *Tetragnatha viridorufa*
   පොදු දිගු හනුක දිය මකුළුවා
   2cm. Nocturnal. Abdomen and pedipalps elongated. Abdomen is green, brown, and red. A well-camouflaged species associated with wetlands.

Plate 44

1. Common Two-tailed Spider *Hersilia sevignyi*
   හර්සිලියා මකුළුවා / පොදු දෙනෙටි මකුළුවා
   2cm. Arboreal. Has a flattened shape. 'Tail' at the end of the abdomen is a key feature in identifying this family.

2. Hermit Spider *Nephilengys malabarensis*
   පොදු වෛරම් නිවෙස් මකුළුවා
   1.5cm. Dorsal side of the body has brown, black colour; ventral side has red spots. Common in 'Kumbuk' trees rivers.

3. Red and silver Dewdrop Spider *Argyrodes flavescens*
   රතු රිදී පිණිබිඳු මකුළුවා
   0.6cm. Cryptoparasitic spider usually lives in other spiders' orb webs. Red and white. Commonly found with Giant Wood Spider.

4. Yellow-striped Lynx Spider *Oxyopes macilentus*
   කහ ඉරි ලින්ක්ස් මකුළුවා
   1.2cm. Diurnal. Legs with long spine-like hairs. Lives in low vegetation. Orange body colour and has white or yellow stripes along abdomen.

5. Grass Funnel-weaver *Tegenaria domestica*
   කේතු දැල් වියන්නා
   1.5cm. Strictly terrestrial, associated with grassy and rocky areas. Has a funnel-shaped retreat. Brown in colour. Funnel size average 30cm.

6. Six-spotted Fishing Spider *Dolomedes (cf.) triton*
   තිත් සයැති දිය මකුළුවා
   1.5cm. Semi-aquatic. Two white bands on sides of body. Six white spots on back.

7. Grass Funnel-web Spider *Hippasa greenalliae*
   විදුලි බිම් හමන්නා
   1cm. Inhabits sandy ground. Brown, grey, and black.

8. Domestic Huntsman Spider *Heteropoda venatoria*
   පුළුන් කොට්ටා මකුළුවා
   2cm. Nocturnal. Spans 10-12cm with legs. Present inside buildings, on logs, tree trunks and stones.

Plate 45

1. **Sri Lanka Elongated Green Crab Spider** *Oxytate subvirens* ●
   ශ්‍රී ලංකා කොළ කකුළු මකුළුවා
   1.2cm. Diurnal. Inhabits leaves on vegetation. Green. Holds first two pairs of legs like a crab.

2. **Common House Fly Catcher** *Plexippus petersi*
   මකුළු මැසිමාරා
   0.8cm. Very common anthropogenic spider. Mostly feeds on houseflies. Diurnal.

3. **White Flower Crab Spider** *Thomisus spectabilis*
   ඇලි කකුළු මකුළුවා
   0.8cm. Diurnal. Holds first two pairs of legs like a crab. Frequently found on flowers but well camouflaged.

4. **Banded Phintella** *Phintella vittata*
   කුරු පිනුම් මකුළුවා
   0.7cm. Diurnal. Luminous blue bands across abdomen. Lives amongst vegetation.

5. **Red & blue Tiny Jumper** *Siler semiglaucus*
   නිල් විසිතුරු පිනුම් මකුළුවා
   0.6cm. Diurnal. Blue, red, and white. Often raises first pair of legs.

6. **Giant Ant-like Jumper** *Myrmarachne maxillosea*
   කළු කඩි මකුළුවා
   1.0cm. Body mimics that of a big black ant. Lives in vegetation. Males have large pedipalps compared to body size.

7. **Red Ant-like Jumper** *Myrmarachne palataleoides*
   දිමි මකුළුවා
   1.0cm. Diurnal. Mimics Red Ant *Ooecoplyla smaragdina*. Males have elongated pedipalps.

8. **Two-striped Telamonia** *Telamonia dimidiata*
   යෝධ දෙඉරි පිනුම් මකුළුවා
   1.4cm. Diurnal. White band along abdomen, white spot on head. Female pale white. Lives in vegetation.

Dragonflies & Damselflies

(Plates 46-50)

Dragonflies and damselflies are insects that belong to the order Odonata. In Sri Lanka a total of 119 odonates, including 56 endemics, are currently known to science. They can be classified under two Sub-orders namely Anisoptera and Zygoptera.

Zygopterans, commonly referred to as damselflies, are generally smaller and delicately-built insects with small hammer shaped head, two well separated compound eyes, and slender abdomen and equally sized narrow wings that are placed along the abdomen when at rest. Anisopterans or dragonflies are usually much larger and have two large compound eyes that touch each other at the center, hind wing that are expanded at the base, and keep their wings broadly opened when at rest.

Odonates have an incomplete metamorphosis and their larval stages are exclusively aquatic. Both damselflies and dragonflies are active carnivores.

In Udawalawe National Park, many dragonflies can be found near rivers, streams, tanks, ponds, and marshes. Some species prefer shade.

Plate 46

1. **Green Skimmer** *Orthetrum sabina*
   Abdomen greenish yellow marked with black. Abdominal segements 1 to 3 distinctively swollen, 4 to 6 cylindrical and thin, 7 to 9 dilated and laterally compressed. Sexes similar. **Abdomen length:** 32-33mm. Very common in open areas and along water bodies.

2. **Dancing Dropwing** *Trithemis pallidinervis*
   Abdomen black marked with bright yellow. **Male:** Front yellow and metallic purple, wings hyaline, anal appendages yellow at base and then black. **Female:** Front metallic golden green, wings tinted with yellow or reddish brown, anal appendages yellow. **Abdomen length:** 30mm (m), 27mm (f). Common around large tanks. Adults often perch on tall reeds.

3. **Pink Skimmer** *Orthetrum pruinosum*
   Thorax reddish brown. Wings hyaline with reddish brown marking in hind wing. **Male:** Abdomen bright vermilion-red to purplish-red. Eyes blue-black above. **Female:** Abdomen dull ochreous, borders finely black. Eyes yellowish capped brown. **Abdomen length:** 29mm (m), 30mm (f). Very common around tanks, ponds, and slow-flowing streams.

4. **Crimson Dropwing** *Trithemis aurora*
   Male: Abdomen pink. Eyes crimson above, sides brown and pink below. Thorax dull purple. Wings hyaline with crimson nervures and amber bases. **Female:** Abdomen yellowish, marked with black. Eyes purplish brown above, lilac or grey below. Thorax yellow green. **Abdomen length:** 21-29mm (m), 19-27mm (f). Common around streams, water channels, and tanks.

5. **Wandering Glider** *Pantala flavescens*
   Abdomen ochreous and dorsal black pyriform spots on segments 8 to 10. **Male:** Red tint dorsally in abdomen. Eyes reddish brown above and rest bluish. Wings hyaline with golden yellow in base of hind wings. **Female:** No red tint in abdomen, eyes olive brown above, hyaline wings. **Abdomen length:** 31-32mm Very common in open habitats. Usually flies several meters above ground and perches vertically.

Plate 47

1. **Sociable Glider** *Tramea limbata*
   Abdomen blood red, last three segments mostly black. Wings hyaline with red nervures towards base. Variable black mark in base of hind wings. **Male:** Anal appendages red. **Female:** Anal appendages yellow. **Abdomen length:** 33mm (m), 32mm (f). Common in open habitats.

2. **Variegated Flutterer** *Rhyothemis variegata*
   Abdomen black. **Male:** Wings fully tinted yellow and marked with black and amber yellow. **Female:** Front wings hyaline from apex to nodes. Hind wing hyaline only at apex, rest is marked more heavily than males with black and yellow. **Abdomen length:** 24mm (m), 21mm (f). Found commonly around tanks. Regularly seen high above ground.

3. **Blue Pursuer** *Potamarcha congener*
   Male: Abdomen and thorax blue. Lateral yellow stripes on abdominal segments 1-8. Yellow markings on thorax of sub-adults. Wings hyaline with brownish tip in apices. **Female:** Abdomen black marked with broad ochreous stripes. Thorax brown with yellow stripes. Abdominal segment 8 has a lateral expansion. Wings similar to males. **Abdomen length:** 30mm (m, f). Common around weedy ponds and marshes.

4. **Asian Pintail** *Acisoma panorpoides*
   Thorax and abdomen sky blue marked with black. Eyes blue. Wings hyaline. Anal appendages white with the border black. **Females:** Pale ochreous with abdominal segments 8-10 fully black. **Abdomen length:** 15-18mm. Common around ponds, tanks, and marshes.

5. **Asian Groundling** *Brachythemis contaminata*
   Male: Abdomen reddish marked dorsally and subdorsally with brown stripes. Eyes violet brown above. Thorax marked with reddish brown stripes. Wings hyaline with orange basal half and pterostigma. **Female:** Abdomen pale olive brown with a mid black stripe. Eyes pale brown above. Thorax pale greenish yellow, a narrow brown stripe along carina. Wings hyaline, base of hind wing and pterostigma pale yellow. Abdomen length: 20mm (m), 19mm (f). Very common around still and slow-flowing waters.

PLATE 48

1. **Oriental Scarlet** *Crocothemis servilia*
   Male: Abdomen blood red with black mid-dorsal carina. Wings hyaline with amber yellow bases. Eyes red above and rest purple. Thorax red. **Female:** Ochreous abdomen, blackish along mid-dorsal carina. Eyes brown above and olivaceous below. Thorax olivaceous-brown. Wings similar to males. **Abdomen length:** 30mm (m), 25-32mm (f). Common species found near stagnant water.

2. **Scarlet Basker** *Urothemis signata*
   Male: Abdomen blood red with dorsal black marks on segments 8 and 9. Thorax dorsally red and laterally olive. Eyes reddish above. Wings hyaline with reddish brown mark in hind wing base. **Female:** Abdomen olive with dorsal black spots. Thorax olive green. Eyes brown above. Wings similar to males but has lighter marks. **Abdomen length:** 27mm (m), 26mm (f). Common around tanks and water channels.

3. **Blue Percher** *Diplacodes trivialis*
   Male: Thorax and abdomen bluish. Last few abdominal segments black with yellow anal appendages. Eyes blue. Wings hyaline with small yellow spot in base of hind wing. **Female:** Thorax yellow. Abdomen black with yellow lateral markings. Eyes reddish brown above. Wings similar to male. **Abdomen length:** 20mm (m,f). Very common.

4. **Black-tipped Percher** *Diplacodes nebulosa*
   Male: Abdomen and thorax blue or blackish. Wings hyaline with tips black. Eyes dark violet above. **Female:** Abdomen black, sides marked with yellow. Prothorax and thorax lemon yellow. Eyes reddish brown. Wings hyaline. **Abdomen length:** 16mm (m), 14mm (f). Found around weedy tanks and marshes.

5. **Rapacious Flangetail** *Ichtinogomphus rapax*
   Abdomen, thorax, and legs black marked with yellow. **Male:** Abdominal segments 8 with a foliate expansion. Wings hyaline. **Female:** Lack foliate expansion, wings with a dark brown basal marking. **Abdomen length:** 52mm (m), 50mm (f). Common around large tanks and ponds. Usually perches horizontally.

PLATE 49

1. **Pied Parasol** *Neurothemis tullia*
   Male: Abdomen black with broad mid-dorsal stripe of cream white. Wings hyaline for apical half, opaque steely black for basal half and white band on the border of black. **Female:** Abdomen yellow with broad black stripe, black beneath. Wing patterns very variable yellow and blackish brown. **Abdomen length:** 18mm (m, f) Very common and usually found in numbers around ponds, tanks, channels and slow flowing streams.

2. **Green's Gem** *Libellago greeni*
   Male: Abdomen black marked with citron yellow and blood red. Wings hyaline with apices of front wings black. **Female:** Abdomen black marked with lemon yellow. Wings hyaline. **Abdomen length:** 14mm (m), 12-13mm (f).

3. **Yellow Waxtail** *Ceriagrion coromandelianum*
   Male: Abdomen bright yellow. Olive green prothorax and thorax. Yellow legs with black spines. Wings hyaline. **Female:** Abdomen olivaceous tinged yellow. Olivaceous brown prothorax and thorax. Legs and wings similar to males. **Abdomen length:** 28-30mm (m), 29-32mm (f). Very common around tanks, ponds, marshes, and streams.

4. **Common Bluetail** *Ischnura senegalensis*
   Male: Abdomen dorsally black with blue on segments 1,2 and 8. Segment 9 laterally blue and 3-7 are yellow laterally. Thorax green. **Female:** Three forms. 1: Similar to male with abdominal segment 9 laterally green. 2: Thorax and abdomen dorsally black and laterally pale flesh. 3: Abdominal segments 1-2 fully orange, lateral sides of 3-7 blue and 8-10 orange. **Abdomen length:** 21-23mm (m), 14-16mm (f) Usually around ponds, tanks and marshes. Females somewhat rare.

5. **Malabar Sprite** *Pseudagrion malabaricum*
   Male: Abdomen and thorax blue with black markings. Superior anal appendages not bifid. Wings hyaline with dark brown pterostigma. **Female:** Similar to male in pattern but more greenish. **Abdomen length:** 33mm (m), 32mm (f) Commonly found around tanks, ponds, and marshes.

Plate 50

1. **Orange-faced Sprite** *Pseudagrion rubriceps*
   Bright orange head. Thorax olive green. Abdomen dorsally black with a bright blue tip. **Female:** Less extensive blue colour in abdomen tip than males. **Abdomen length:** 32mm (m), 29mm (f). A common species. Found along the edges of bodies of water.

2. **Wandering Wisp** *Agriocnemis pygmaea*
   Male: Abdomen segments 1-6 greenish yellow, rest red. Anal appendages red. Thorax dorsally black with green laterally. **Female:** Three forms. 1: Similar to male but abdominal segments 2-6 laterally yellow. 2: Abdominal segments 1-7 red laterally. 3: Greenish abdomen with segments 8-10 yellow. **Abdomen length:** 16-17mm (m), 18mm (f) One of the smallest damselflies in Sri Lanka. Common around weedy tanks, ponds, and marshes.

3. **Ultima Gem** *Libellago finalis*
   Male: Abdomen black with citron yellow markings except on segments 8-10. Head, thorax black with yellow-yellowish green marks. Wings hyaline with amber-tinted base. Apices of forewings black. **Female:** Markings present on segment 8-10. A large round spot on segment 9. Wings slightly tinted with cream white pterostigma. **Abdomen length:** 16mm. Common around streams and rivers with shade.

4. **Yellow Featherleg** *Copera marginipes*
   Male: Thorax bronze black with greenish yellow lines. Abdomen black with white tip. Base of segments 3-7 white. Yellow legs. **Female:** Paler than males. Abdomen varies from dark brown to white. Apical dark marks in segment 3-7. **Abdomen length:** 34mm (m), 30mm (f). Common. Found on low vegetation around ponds and streams. Sometimes keeps wings spread when at rest.

5. **Indian Rockdweller** *Bradinopyga geminata*
   Both sexes: Thorax bluish grey. Abdomen black with distinctive yellow markings. Anal appendages yellow. Wings hyaline. Pterostigma entirely black or black with white spots on either side. Eyes reddish brown above. **Abdomen length:** 19mm (m,f). Well camouflaged. Commonly found on granite rocks beside rock pools.

Butterflies
(Plates 51-61)

Butterflies are instantly recognized by people the world over as attractive, harmless, insects. They are found in every habitat from mountaintops to the darkest jungle, in desert and in our gardens - a truly cosmopolitan group.

Butterflies and moths belong to the order Lepidoptera, a name that points to the principal characteristics of this group: it derives from the Greek word *lepis*, meaning "scale", and *pteron*, "wing". The presence of overlapping scales on the wings and body helps distinguish the Lepidoptera from other insects orders. Their closest relatives are the caddisflies (Order Trichoptera), which have wings covered by scale-like hairs.

The Lepidoptera manifest metamorphosis during their 'birth'. The transformation from caterpillar to pupa and then to a large-winged, often brightly coloured, butterfly is dramatic.

The Lepidoptera order is one of the biggest in Phylum Insecta, with an estimated 200,000 species.

Butterflies are today strongly associated with flowering plants, and it is likely that plants and butterflies co-evolved.

There are 245 known butterfly species in Sri Lanka in 5 families; 26 of then are endemic to the Sri Lanka.

Plate 51

1. **Sri Lanka Birdwing** *Troides darsius* ●
   10-13cm. Largest butterfly in Sri Lanka. Common in riverine areas. Flies at medium speed.

2. **Crimson Rose** *Pachliopta hector*
   9-10cm. Very common. Abundant in open grassland near tanks. Flies at medium speed.

3. **Common Rose** *Pachliopta aristolochiae*
   8.5cm. Common. Occurs in vegetation edges and open areas. Medium speed flight.

4. **Banded Peacock** *Papilio crino*
   8cm. Rare. Mostly in drier parts, fairly fast flight, one of the most beautiful butterfly.

5. **Lime Butterfly** *Papilio demoleus*
   8-9cm. Common. Prefers dry areas. Fast flight.

6. **Blue Mormon** *Papilio polymnestor*
   12cm. Large butterfly. Very common. Slow flight.

7. **Mine** *Chilasa clytia*
   10cm. Fairly uncommon. Medium speed flight, two colour forms present.

8. **Psyche** *Leptosia nina*
   4cm. Very common. Flies very slowly in lower vegetation.

9. **Jezebel** *Delias eucharis*
   7-8cm. Common. May be confused with the Painted Saw-tooth. Flies at medium speed.

10. **Pioneer** *Belenois aurota*
    4-5cm. Common. May be confused with the Common Gull. Flies fast.

PLATE 52

1. Common Gull *Cepora nerissa*
   4.5-5cm. Common. May be confused with the Pioneer. Fast flight.

2. Common Albatross *Appias albina*
   5-6cm. Fairly common. Migratory. Fast flight.

3. White Orange-tip *Ixias marianne*
   4.5-5.5cm. Uncommon. Prefers thorny areas. Flies at medium speed.

4. Great Orange-tip *Hebomoia glaucippe*
   8-9cm. Fairly rare. Mid-elevation flyer mainly in the sub-canopy level. Medium fast flight.

5. Mottled Immigrant *Catopsilia pyranthe*
   4-6cm. Very common. Migratory. Fast flight.

6. Dark Wanderer *Pareronia ceylanica*
   6-7cm. Fairly common. Flies at shrub level. Medium fast flight.

7. Small Salmon-arab *Colotis amata*
   3.5-4cm. Common. Flying at a low height. Medium fast flight.

8. Little Orange-tip *Colotis etrida*
   3-4cm. Uncommon. Flies in low vegetation. Fast flight.

9. Small Grass-yellow *Eurema brigitta*
   3-4cm. Rare. Inner black patch pattern distinctive. Medium fast flight.

10. Common Grass-yellow *Eurema hecabe*
    4-4.5cm. Common. May be confused with Three-spot Grass Yellow. Medium speed flight.

Plate 53

1. Three-spot Grass-yellow *Eurema blanda*
   4.5cm. Common. Mottled wings. Medium fast flight.

2. Tree Nymph *Idea iasonia*
   13cm. Uncommon. Found near rivers. Very slow flight with frequent glides.

3. Glassy Tiger *Parantica aglea*
   7-7.5cm. Very common. Ubiquitous. Slow flight.

4. Plain Tiger *Danaus chrysippus*
   7-8cm. Common. Mostly occurs in open areas. Medium fast flight.

5. Common Crow *Euploea core*
   8.5cm. Very common in thick vegetation. Low-level flyer. Slow flight.

6. Tawny Castor *Acraea violae*
   5.5-6cm. Very common. Prefers open areas. Weak and slow flight.

7. Angled Castor *Ariadne ariadne*
   4.5cm. Uncommon. Abundant in grassy areas with rocks. Medium speed flight.

8. Rustic *Cupha erymanthis*
   5.5-6cm. Common. Inhabits lower vegetation. Medium fast flight.

9. Leopard *Phalanta phalantha*
   5-5.5cm. Common. Frequent in scrub. Fast flight.

10. Cruiser *Vindula erota*
    8.5-10cm. Fairly uncommon. Associated with moist forest areas. Medium flight.

Plate 54

1. Tamil Yeoman *Cirrochroa thais*
   6cm. Common. Frequent in scrub. Medium speed flight.

2. Lace Wing *Cethosia nietneri*
   8.5-9cm. Uncommon. Flies at medium height. Flies at medium speed.

3. Painted Lady *Vanessa cardui*
   5-5.5cm. Associated with wet soil in dry areas but rare. Flies fast.

4. Grey Pansy *Junonia atlites*
   5.5cm. Very common. Prefers open grassland and vegetation edges. Medium fast flight.

5. Peacock Pansy *Junonia almana*
   4.5cm. Common. Usually found open grassland. Fast flight.

6. Danaid Eggfly *Hypolimnas misippus*
   7cm. Uncommon. Inhibits forested areas. Medium fast flight.

7. Sri Lanka Blue Oakleaf *Kallima philarchus* 🟢
   8-9.5cm. Very rare. Occurs in deep forest areas with rivers or streams. Medium fast flight.

8. Common Sailor *Neptis hylas*
   4.5-5cm. Very common. Common in low vegetation. Slow flight.

9. Chestnut-streaked Sailor *Neptis jumbah*
   6-6.5cm. Fairly common. Associated with river banks. Flight slow.

10. Commander *Moduza procris*
    6cm. Uncommon. Occurs at mid-canopy level in forest. Slow flight.

Plate 55

1. Clipper *Parthenos sylvia*
   9cm. Fairly uncommon. Occurs inside forest from mid- to upper canopy. Slow flight.

2. Baron *Euthalia aconthea*
   5-6cm. Uncommon. Usually inhibits dark, shaded areas in forest. Fast flyer.

3. Black Prince *Rohana parisatis*
   3.5-4cm. Rare. Occurs in rocky areas in the middle of the day. Very fast flight.

4. Nawab *Polyura athamas*
   5-6cm. Rare. Canopy specialist. Hard to spot. Extremely fast flight.

5. Tawny Rajah *Charaxes psaphon*
   7-9cm. Very rare. Canopy dweller. Fast flight.

6. Common Eveningbrown *Melannitis leda*
   6.5cm. Common. Frequents undergrowth. Hard to detect. Slow flight.

7. Common Treebrown *Lethe rohria*
   6cm. Fairly common. Prefers shaded areas under dense forest canopy. Fast flight.

8. Nigger *Orsotriaena medus*
   4cm. Very common. Usually perched on ground or on a dead leaf. Slow flight.

9. Common Bushbrown *Mycalesis perseus*
   4cm. Common. Occurs in undergrowth with leaf litter. Slow and low level flyer.

10. White Four-ring *Ypthima ceylonica*
    3cm. Very common. Lives close to ground level. Slow flight.

Plate 56

1. Common Palmfly *Elymnias hypermnestra*
   6.5cm. Common. Associated with palm trees. Female mimics Common Tiger, Slow flight.

2. Apefly *Spalgis epeus*
   2.3cm. Fairly uncommon. Larvae eat mealy bugs. Fast flight.

3. Indian Sunbeam *Curetis thetis*
   3.5-4cm. Uncommon. Prefers mid-level vegetation. Fast flight.

4. Centaur Oakblue *Arhopala pseudocentaurus*
   5-5.2cm. Uncommon. Prefers canopy. Fast flight.

5. Common Acaciablue *Surendra vivarna*
   3.1cm. Uncommon. Prefers thorny scrubs. Medium-fast flight.

6. Redspot *Zesius chrysomallus*
   4cm. Uncommon. Flies during mid-day hours. Very fast flight.

7. Purple Leafblue *Amblypodia anita*
   4.3-5cm. Rare. Around puddles of water. Fast flight.

8. Common Tinsel *Catapaecilma major*
   2.9-3.1cm. Very rare. Hops from bush to bush. Slow flight.

9. Yamfly *Loxura atymnus*
   3.3-3.5cm. Uncommon. Occurs in riverine areas with dense canopy. Slow, gentle flight.

10. Monkey Puzzle *Rathinda amor*
    2.3-2.8cm. Common. Prefers the lower levels of vegetation. Medium speed flight.

PLATE 57

1. Common Imperial *Cheritra freja*
   3.6cm. Rare. Prefers riverine areas. Medium-fast flight.

2. Common Silverline *Spindasis vulcanus*
   2.5cm. Common. Prefers drier areas of open ground. Fast flight.

3. Nilgiri Tit *Hypolycaena nilgirica*
   2.4cm. Rare. Prefers low level vegetation. Medium-fast flight.

4. Plane *Bindahara phocides*
   3-3.5cm. Rare. Prefers dense forest. Medium flight speed.

5. Common Guavablue *Virachola isocrates*
   4cm. Common. Prefers mid-level vegetation. Fast flight.

6. Cornelian *Deudorix epijarbas*
   3.6-3.8cm. Rare. Sunbathes in the morning. Fast flight.

7. Pointed Ciliateblue *Anthene lycaenina*
   2.5cm. Fairly uncommon. Occurs in vegetation edges. Fast flight.

8. Dingy Lineblue *Petrelaea dana*
   2-2.5cm. Fairly common. Around puddles. Medium-fast flight.

9. Sri Lanka Pale 6 - Lineblue *Nacaduba sinhala* ●
   2.6-2.8cm. Rare. Shaded areas in forest. Fast flight.

10. Common Lineblue *Prosotas nora*
    2.2cm. Common. Forest. Medium-fast flight.

Plate 58

1. Dark Cerulean *Jamides bochus*
   2.8cm. Uncommon. Inhabits edges of vegetation. Fast flight.

2. Metallic Cerulean *Jamides alecto*
   3.2cm. Uncommon. Shaded areas in forest. Fast flight.

3. Common Cerulean *Jamides celeno*
   3.1cm. Common. Ubiquitous. Medium flight.

4. Forget-me-not *Catochrysops strabo*
   2.8cm. Uncommon. Open grasslands. Medium flight speed.

5. Pea Blue *Lampides boeticus*
   2.7-3cm. Very common. Dry Zone. Medium flight speed.

6. Zebra Blue *Syntarucus plinius*
   2.5cm. Fairly common. Congregates around puddles. Medium fast flight.

7. Common Pierrot *Castalius rosimon*
   2.5-2.8cm. Very common in plains. Medium fast flight.

8. Grass Jewel *Freyeria trochilus*
   1.7cm. Common. Smallest butterfly in Sri Lanka. Grassland and open country.

9. Lesser Grassblue *Zizina otis*
   2cm. Very common. Open areas. Fast flight.

10. Tiny Grassblue *Zizula hylax*
    1.8-2cm. Common. Open areas. Fast flight.

PLATE 59

1. Red Pierrot *Talicada nyseus*
   3-3.2cm. Uncommon. Flies near to ground. Slow flight.

2. Indian Cupid *Everes lacturnus*
   2.5cm. Common. Tall grassy areas. Medium flight.

3. Common Hedgeblue *Actyolepis puspa felderi*
   2.8cm. Uncommon. Frequents bird droppings. Fast flight.

4. Quaker *Neopithicops zalmora*
   2.3cm. Uncommon. Seen on bird droppings. Fast flight.

5. Malayan *Megisba malaya*
   2cm. Uncommon. Rests on bird droppings. Fast flight.

6. Gram Blue *Euchrysops cnejus*
   2.5-2.9cm. Uncommon. Low vegetation. Fast flight.

7. Lime Blue *Chilades lajus*
   Uncommon. In low vegetation. Larva feeds on citrus; red ants appear to gain sustenance from the larva and defend it with their lives. Medium speed flight.

8. Plum Judy *Abisara echerius*
   4-4.2cm. Common. Prefers low vegetation.

PLATE 60

HESPERIIDAE
(Skippers, Darts, and Flats)

1. Branded Orange Awlet *Bibasis oedipodea ataphus*
2. Brown Awl *Badamia exclamationis*
3. Giant Redeye *Gangara thyrsis clothilda*
4. Sri Lanka Black Flat *Celaenorrhinus spilothyrus* 🟢
5. Tricolour Pied Flat *Coladenia indrani*
6. Common Small Flat *Sarangesa dasahara aibicilia*
7. Ceylon Snow Flat *Tagiades japetus obscurus*
8. Golden Angle *Caprona ransonnettii ransonnettii*
9. Bush Hopper *Amittia dioscorides singa*
10. Indian Palm Bob *Suastus gremius subgrisea*
11. Chestnut Bob *Iambrix salsala luteipalpus*
12. Common Banded Demon *Notocrypta paralysos alysia*
13. Tree Flitter *Hyarotis adrastus*
14. Common Redeye *Matapa aria*
15. Indian Skipper *Spalia galba*

Plate 61

1. Common Grassdart *Taractrocera maevius*
2. Common Dartlet *Oriens goloides*
3. Tropic Dart *Potanthus confuscius satra*
4. Pale Palmdart *Telicota colon amba*
5. Conjoined Swift *Pelopidas conjuncta narooa*
6. Smallest Swift *Parnara bada bada*

Fishes
(Plates 62-67)

Fishes are distinct from other vertebrates owing to their aquatic lifestyle, the presence of scales on their bodies, and possession of fins that are used for propulsion. They use oxygen that is dissolved in water. The sensory system is usually based on the 'lateral line', a series of tiny pores along the body that are sensitive to chemical, electrical, and pressure stimuli. Some bottom-dwelling species have sensitive barbs that alert them to ambient conditions.

PLATE 62

1. **Halfbeak** *Zenarchopterus dispar*
   මොරැල්ලා
   15cm. Grey brown dorsally, silvery on sides, with a broad black streak running the length of the side. Anal and dorsal fins displaced posteriorly, dark blotch on dorsal fin. Caudal fin truncate. Lower jaw elongate and pointed. Upper jaw shorter.

2. **Stinging Catfish** *Heteropneustes fossilis*
   හුංගා
   20-30cm. Shape similar to *Clarias brachysoma* (S.: Magura). Dorsal fin very small. Four pairs elongate barbels, very elongate base to anal fin. Sides grey brown, becoming darker dorsally. May have two vague, yellowish lateral bands on sides. Colour varies from dark bottle green to yellowish, black or rust brown. Juveniles copper or reddish brown referred to in Sinhala as 'Rathu hunga' or 'Lay hunga'. Prefers aquatic vegetation and muddy waters.

3. **Butter Catfish** *Ompok bimaculatus*
   වලපොත්තා
   40cm. Laterally compressed, mouth wide. Belly white and convex, mustard yellow. More greenish dorsally, with dark brown mottles on the dorsal and lateral surfaces. Younger juveniles (< 2 cm) are almost totally transparent.

4. **Striped Dwarf Catfish** *Mystus vittatus*
   ඉරි අංකුට්ටා
   10cm. Dorsal fin more rounded, have lateral longitudinal stripe. Dorsal surface greenish brown and sides lighter brown. Ventral surface white. Three of four dark brown stripes along sides, a dark spot on the caudal peduncle.

5. **Bar-eyed Goby** *Glossogobius giuris*
   මහ වැලිගොව්වා
   25cm. Olive dorsally, lightening to a greenish yellow laterally. Several dark spots on side of head and two rows of blotches on the sides. Fins have dark edges and are spotted. Operculum scaled, but cheeks lack scales. Ventral fins fused to help attach surface. Found in water bodies with sandy bottoms.

PLATE 63

1. **Sri Lanka Stone Sucker** *Garra ceylonensis* ●
   ශ්‍රී ලංකා ගල් පාඬියා
   8cm. Brown, lighter on the sides belly white. Mustard colored streak along the side. Two pairs of barbles. Mouth sub-terminal. Prefers flowing water and stays attached to rocky surface. Found in rivers.

2. **Brown Snakehead** *Chamma gachua*
   පරඬැල් කනයා
   15.4cm. Dorsal and caudal fins have orange margins. The caudal fin has blue green rays. Pelvic fin small. Young up to about 1cm in length, dull orange. Prefers waters with vegetation or bottom debris.

3. **Spotted Snakehead** *Channa punctata*
   මඩ කනයා
   15cm. Dorsal surface olive green to brown. Sides and fins brownish yellow. Ventral surface off-white. Several dark blotches along sides; indistinct dark bars between dorsal fin and the lateral line. Dorsum has four to five rows of spots. Dark spot at base of pectoral fin. Young dark brown with three yellow stripes on sides. Prefers muddy water.

4. **Murrel** *Channa striata*
   ලුලා
   75cm. Bright olive green dorsally. White ventrally, several oblique, green-brown bars along sides. Fins olive. Juveniles initially colourless but, later, bright orange. Large fish. Prefers tanks with aquatic vegetation.

Plate 64

1. **Orange Chromide** *Etroplus maculatus*
   කහ කොරලියා
   7cm. Heavily compressed, disc-shaped body. Sides brownish yellow, darker dorsally. Tiny red dots along sides. One to five dark blotches on sides. Ventral side turn inky black when frightened. Bright blue half-circle ringing lower part of eye. Found in pairs.

2. **Pearl Spot** *Etroplus suratensis*
   කොරලියා
   30cm. Greyish green on sides, darker dorsally. Six to eight dark bars on sides and forehead. Dark spot at base of pectoral fin. Scales on upper part of sides have bright spot. Irregular black dots on lower body, between pectoral and anal fins.

3. **Giant Gourami** *Osphronemus goramy*
   සෙජ්පිලි / තිත්පිලියා / යෝධ ගුරාමියා
   25cm. Body strongly compressed. One ray of pelvic fin extends into filament. Dorsal side dark grey, sides lighter. Juveniles have dark vertical bands on sides. Anal fins tinged with pink. With dark blotch below lateral line under posterior extremity of dorsal fin and at base of pectoral fin. Can breathe atmospheric air. Introduced.

4. **Tilapia** *Oreochromis mossambicus*
   තිලාපියා / තෙත්පිලියා / ජපන් බට්ටා / බට්ටා
   35cm. No conspicuous color pattern. Sides dull brown to olive green or dull gold. Dorsal side darker. Caudal fin with orange margin. Juveniles have black spot at posterior end of dorsal fin. Few dark blotches on sides. Introduced invasive.

5. **Tilapia** *Oreochromis niloticus*
   තිලාපියා
   40cm. Have regular and definite stripes on caudal fin, dark margin on dorsal. Hazy dark bars on sides. Breeding males flushed with red. Mouthbrooder.

PLATE 65

1. Silver Carplet *Amblypharyngodon melettinus*
   සොරයා
   8cm. Greenish grey dorsally, sides light golden. Fins greyish and translucent. No prominent markings on body. Broad lateral stripe. Lateral line incomplete. Introduced.

2. Giant Danio *Devario malabaricus*
   රත් කයියා / දම්කොළ සාලයා
   8cm. Grey-brown dorsally and metallic blue on the sides. Ventral surface white. Two minute pairs of barbels. Two to three yellow stripes along sides breaking into spots. Short vertical bars anteriorly. Fins usually yellow.

3. Sri Lanka Flying Barb *Esomus thernoicos* 🟢
   ශ්‍රී ලංකා රැවුල් දණ්ඩියා
   6-10cm. Has very long pair of maxillary barbles trailing up to ventrals. Barbles whitish. Dorsal surface olive grey, sides silvery with two parallel stripes, one blue-black and the other yellow. Some have red or orange tint on caudal fin. Prefers clear waters.

4. Stripped Rasbora *Rasbora microchephala*
   කිරි දණ්ඩියා
   10cm. Looks like *R. dandia* but has a narrower and smoother lateral stripe. Distance from the base of the first dorsal ray to hypural (or caudal peduncle). less than that from first dorsal ray base to eye.

5. Common Labeo *Labeo dussumieri*
   හිරි කනයා
   40cm. Dorsal surface and fins golden brown. Sides lighter. Has two pairs of barbels. Ventral profile rounded. Large spot on caudal peduncle. The scales of the shoulder region of breeding males have red edging.

6. Rohu *Labeo rohita*
   රෝහු
   1m. Small, subterminal mouth, red fins. When mature, body deep red. One pair of barbels. Introduced.

PLATE 66

1. **Sri lanka Olive Barb** *Systomus timbiri* 🟢
   ශ්‍රී ලංකා මස් පෙතියා
   30cm. A plain fish. Dorsally olive brown, laterally silvery with pronounced scales. Dark spot on caudal peduncle. Has two pairs of barbels. Juveniles have a black spot on body, just below the dorsal fin. Considerable variations in depth and width of body.

2. **Sri lanka Filamented Barb** *Dawkinsia sinhala* 🟢
   ශ්‍රී ලංකා දම්කොළ පෙතියා
   10-12cm. Changes colouring as it matures. Juveniles up to about 2cm. Have three black bars on sides. Dorsal surface is dull green-brown, sides are silvery. In adult no dark patch beneath the dorsal fin. Blotch anterior to caudal peduncle becomes horizontally elongate oval. Red tinge on caudal fin turns to black. During mating dorsal fins of males develop elongate rays that may reach up to caudal peduncle. Body becomes tinged with green and red on sides.

3. **Redside Barb** *Puntius bimaculatus*
   ඉපිලි කඩයා
   4-7cm. Has silvery sides with a bright crimson band that extends along lateral line to posterior of caudal fin. Black spot at base of the dorsal fin and on the caudal peduncle. One short pair of barbles.

4. **Silver Barb** *Puntius vittatus*
   බණ්ඩි තිත්තයා
   3-4cm. Dorsal side of this fish is pale olive and the sides are silvery. Has oblique black band edged with orange or yellow on the dorsal fin and black spot on caudal peduncle. Another very small black spot on ventral side near anterior extremity of anal fin.

5. **Sri Lanka Swamp Barb** *Puntius thermalis* 🟢
   ශ්‍රී ලංකා කොට පෙතියා
   8-15cm. Elongate fish. One pair barbels. Has black spot about size of eye. Two scale widths in diameters on the aniterior portion of caudal. Body silvery, scales pronounced. Fins yellow may be tinged with orange. Some adults have red-green colouring along sides.

PLATE 67

1. **Long-snouted Barb** *Puntius dorsalis*
   කටු පෙතියා
   25cm. Greenish brown dorsally, sides golden. A faint black blotch on caudal peduncle. Dorsal fin has sharp, strong spine. Juveniles have black spot at base of dorsal fin and fainter one on the caudal penduncle.

2. **Mahseer** *Tor khudree*
   ලෙහෙල්ලා
   1m. Olive brown dorsally and silvery on sides. Tails may be a delicate blue. Pectoral and pelvic fins edged with white or light orange. Four relatively long barbels. Thick-lipped and the thin-lipped varieties co-exist in the same waters, and differentiation appears to be not sexual.

3. **Grass Carp** *Ctenopharyngodon idella*
   තණකොළ කාපයා
   75cm. An elongate, full-bodied, typically carp-like fish. Dorsally grayish, sides being silvery. No barbels. Mouth small. Fins usually grey to black and scales large. Introduced.

4. **Mrigal** *Cirrhinus mrigala*
   මිරිගල්
   40cm. Typical carp-like fish. Caudal fin deeply forked. Upper jaw ends slightly before lower. One pair of short rostral barbels. Dorsally grey, lightening below the lateral line. The ventral and anal fins may be tipped with orange. Introduced.

5. **Catla** *Catla catla*
   කැටීලා
   2m. Deep, unusually-shaped body. Thick lips and eyes set well forward in the head. Upper part of body dark grey, becoming silvery below lateral line. Fins usually dark grey or black. Introduced.

Amphibians

(Plates 68-69)

Amphibians are thought to have been the first vertebrates to have evolved to live away from water. These animals are capable of living both in water and on land. Modern amphibians breathe through their skins and require moist habitats to survive. Despite this specialized requirement, amphibians have evolved into over 250 genera and 2000+ species around the world.

Sri Lanka is represented by 111 species belonging to seven families. When Prof. Keerthisinghe first surveyed Sri Lanka's amphibians in 1956 he was able to name only 39 species. However, through the years, specially during the last 20 years, we have seen a surge of new species identified in Family Rhacophoridae (tree/bush frogs) some of which are visually spectacular.

In Sri Lanka approximately 35% of frog species do not show a 'tadpole' stage. Instead, they develop within an egg and 'froglets', tiny adult frogs, hatch out. This phenomenon is called 'direct development'.

The total number of frog species in Sri Lanka is 111. They belong to the families Bufonidae, Dicroglossidae, Microhylidae, Nyctibatrachidae, Ranidae, Rhacophoridae, and Icthyophidae. Nearly 65% of Sri Lanka's frogs belong to the Rhacophoridae.

Plate 68

1. **Common Toad** *Duttaphrynus melanostictus*
   ගෙයි ගෙම්බා
   Male: 50.3–90.0mm., Female: 70.0–95.0mm. Colour variable - olive, brown or brick red - venter whitish-brown with brown spots. Entirely terrestrial, widely distributed in Sri Lanka.

2. **Common Bull Frog** *Kaloula taprobanica*
   විසිතුරු රතු මැඩියා
   56.4mm. Globular in shape, snout short. Dorsally reddish-orange, venter pale yellowish-grey. Spotted with dark brown or black. This burrowing frog is found on wet leaf litter.

3. **Ornate Narrow-mouth Frog** *Microhyla ornata*
   විසිතුරු මුව පටු මැඩියා
   Mature males: 17.0-22.0mm., Females: 22.0-25.0mm. Head broader than long, bluntly pointed snout. Dorsally light brown with pinkish-olive or grey markings. Belly whitish-yellow. Found in leaf litter in the daytime.

4. **Red Narrow-mouth Frog** *Microhyla rubra*
   රතු මුව පටු මැඩියා
   Mature males: 20.0-27.5mm., Females 20.5-29.5mm. Head broader than long. Snout rounded and short. Dorsally light brown or reddish-brown, a black lateral band from tip of snout through eye to groin, belly white. Common in the Dry Zone. Found in leaf litter in the daytime.

5. **White-bellied Pug-snout Frog** *Ramanella variegata*
   බඩ සුදු මොට හොඹු මැඩියා
   35.0mm. Head broader than long, snout short. Dorsal colour pale brown with olive or irregular dark brown patches, belly white with pale brown spots. Found on the rough bark of trees, in crevices, and humid places in houses, eg., toilets.

6. **Indian Skipper Frog** *Euphlyctis cyanophlyctis*
   උත්පතන මැඩියා
   Mature males: 35.0-45.0mm., Females: 50.0-65.0mm. Snout bluntly pointed. Dorsally brownish or olive brown, spotted. This frog is especially well adapted to aquatic life and is active both during day and night.

PLATE 69

1. Six-toed Green Frog *Euphlyctis hexadactylus*
   සයැගිලි පලා මැඩියා
   Mature males: 58.0-86.8mm., Females: 58.5-120.0mm. Head is longer than it is broad. Dorsal surface bright green or mud-brown. Belly pale yellow or creamy white. Purely aquatic, common and widely distributed in reservoirs, rivers, and marshes.

2. Jerdon's Bull Frog *Hoplobatrachus crassus*
   ජඩන්ගේ දිය මැඩියා
   Mature males: 65.0-80.0mm., Females: 75.0-121.0mm. Head is longer than it is broader. Dorsal colour brown or greenish brown, belly white. Inhabits large water bodies, slow flowing channels, and swamps.

3. Common Hour-glass Tree frog *Polypedates cruciger*
   සුලබ පහිඹු ගස් මැඩියා
   Mature males: 50.0-59.8mm., Females: 72.0-90.0mm. Dorsally pale brownish orange, a dark brown hourglass-shaped marking mid-dorsum. Belly white. This is an entirely arboreal species found in human-occupied habitats and wet woody areas.

4. Spotted Tree frog *Polypedates maculatus*
   පුල්ලි ගස් මැඩියා
   Mature males: 34.5-45.7mm., Females: 43.5-70.0mm. Head longer than it is broad or equal. Dorsal colour olivaceous to chestnut. It is found in human-modified habitats such as houses.

5. Common Paddyfield Frog *Fejervarya limnocharis*
   වෙල් මැඩියා
   Mature males: 19.2-37.0mm., Female: 23.0-50.0mm. Head longer than it is broad. Snout blunt. Dorsally greenish or grayish olive. Abundant in the vicinity of water bodies.

6. Sri Lanka Wood frog *Haylarana gracilis* ●
   ශ්‍රී ලංකා දිය මැඩියා
   Mature males: 32.3–53.7mm., Females: 53.5-67.6mm. Head longer than broad. Dorsally pinkish light brown. A yellowish golden stripe extends from the upper lip to region of the groin. Semi-arboreal. Usually found on wet grasses around water bodies.

Reptiles

(Plates 70-75)

Reptiles are 'cold blooded'. which means that they require multiple strategies to keep themselves alive. The common sight of snakes, lizards, and crocodiles basking in the sun all have to do with this need. Reptiles possess dry skins that are often scaly. Snakes shed their skins regularly to facilitate growth.

Reptiles lay eggs which they do not normally hatch. However, Pythons are known to wrap their body around their eggs to promote hatching. The babies that come out of the eggs are similar to adults in all respects except for the small size.

They are represented on Earth by four main groups: the Chelonians or tortoises and turtles, the Squamata or snakes and lizards, the Crocodilia, and the Tuatara of New Zealand.

PLATE 70

1. **Rock Python** *Python molurus*
   පිඹුරා
   7.6m. Brown and off white (buff). Clear markings on the body are dark grey/brown, reticulate or squarish. Head lance-shaped. Non-venomous. Unmistakable.

2. **Green Vine Snake** *Ahaetulla nasuta*
   ඇහැටුල්ලා
   2m. Long slim grass green. Long head with snout extended out. Dark black/yellow markings on the neck and fore body area seen when puffed up. Has the habit of shaking the fore part of the body from side to side. Mildly venomous.

3. **Buff-striped Keelback** *Amphiesma stolatum*
   අහරකුක්කා
   80cm. Brown and slender with two light buff coloured lines the body from head to tail. Cylindrical head. Non-venomous.

4. **Beddome's Cat Snake** *Boiga beddomei*
   කහ මාපිලා
   1.3m. Arboreal. Head triangular. Vertebral scales strongly enlarged. 19 mid-dorsal scale rows; subcaudal scales number 113-127; dorsum greyish-brown with dark brown vertebral spots; venter yellowish-cream. Mildly venomous.

5. **Olive Keelback** *Atretium schistosum*
   දිය වර්ණා / කඩොලා
   1m. Slim long snake. Cylindrical head. Yellowish brown to greenish brown/yellow dorsal surface, much lighter ventral surface of the same colour.

6. **Forsten's Cat Snake** *Boiga forsteni*
   කබර මාපිලා / ලේ මාපිලා / නාග මාපිලා
   1.7m. Long snake with partial triangular head. Body colour brown, with vertical white markings interspaced with darker brown areas. Eye pupil distinct and vertical. Head has a central dark marking. A dark marking from the eyes backwards to base of head. Mildly venomous.

7. **Sri Lanka Flying Snake** *Chrysopelea taprobanica* ●
   ශ්‍රී ලංකා දගරදන්ඩා
   1m. Slender long body with cylindrical head. Dark sandy brown with clear black bands across the body. Head has transverse black-brown marks. Mildly venomous.

Plate 71

1. **Trinket Snake** *Coelognathus helena*
   කටකළුවා
   1.3m. Cylindrical head. Dorsal area dark sandy brown. Whitish ventral area, separated from the dark brown dorsal surface by a clear black line from mid body to tail. Neck has two dark lines or white collar with dark edges. Non-venomous.

2. **Common Bronzeback Tree Snake** *Dendrelaphis tristis*
   තුරු හාල්දණ්ඩා
   1.5m. Slim long body. Dark sandy brown body. Dorsal brown and whitish ventral separated by blackish brown line from mid body backwards to tail. Head plain brown.

3. **Common Rat Snake** *Ptyas mucosa*
   ගැරඩියා
   3m. Robust long body with distinct neck and prominant head, has large eyes. Dark ashy black to greenish in colour. Faint bar pattern present in juveniles, Second largest snake in Sri Lanka. Non-venomous.

4. **Checkered Keelback** *Xenochrophis piscator*
   දිය නයා / දිය පොළඟා
   1.5m. Slender body, cylindrical head. Body yellowish brown with black cross-like markings hence the "checkered" name. Round pupil. Black line from eye to upper lip.

5. **Russell's Viper** *Daboia russelii*
   තිත් පොළඟා
   1.8m. Stocky, long body, triangular head. Body reddish brown with dark rectangular markings along the dorsal surface. Highly venomous.

6. **Spectacled Cobra** *Naja naja*
   නයා / නාගයා
   2m. Slender long body with almost unclear head. General body colour shiny black dorsally and whitish below. Clear ඏ mark seen only when hood is puffed up. Highly venomous.

7. **Hump-nosed Pit Viper** *Hypnale hypnale*
   කුණ කටුවා / පොළොන් තෙළිස්සා
   56cm. Stocky, long body, triangular head. Head ends with an elongated snout component. Body dark brown to reddish brown. Darker markings across the body. Venomous.

Plate 72

1. **Common Garden Lizard** *Calotes versicolor*
   ගරා කටුස්සා
   SVL 10-12cm; TL 22-27cm. Apices of lateral body scales point upwards. Colour mostly brownish (extremely diverse). Most females with 2 longitudinal, light coloured lines from eye to tail, black shoulder patch. Breeding males with red gular sac. Juveniles light brown with dark transverse lines on body and tail.

2. **Green Garden Lizard** *Calotes calotes*
   පලා කටුස්සා
   SVL 12-13cm, TL 40-41cm. Apices of lateral body scales point upwards. Dorsally bright green with 4-6 transverse bluish white or dark green bands. Yellowish to dark bluish-green head. Breeding males with red or dark red head and gular sac, black shoulder patch. Juveniles mostly bright or light green.

3. **Sri Lanka Painted-lip Lizard** *Calotes ceylonensis* ●
   ශ්‍රී ලංකා තොල් විසිතුරු කටුස්සා
   SVL 7.5-8.5cm; TL 16-18cm. Apices of lateral body scales point backwards. Lips white, pink, orange or red in colour; blackish-brown on anterior part of the body. Darker cross bands on body. Black throat in adult males. Ventrals smaller than dorsals; scales on ventral thigh smooth.

4. **Sri Lanka Lowland Kangaroo Lizard** *Otocryptis nigristigma* ●
   ශ්‍රී ලංකා පිනුම් කටුස්සා / ශ්‍රී ලංකා තැලි කටුස්සා
   SVL 5-8cm; TL 15-17cm. Head appears large. Dark brown. Hind legs longer than fore legs. Male: Gular patch orange with black center. A distinctly black patch present laterally on dewlaps of males.

PLATE 73

1. **Bark Gecko** *Hemidactylus leschenaultii*
   කිඹුල් හූනා / ගස් හූනා
   SVL 7.5-9cm; TL 7-8.5cm. Greyish in colour usually with dark long markings along back.

2. **Sri Lanka Kandyan Gecko** *Hemidactylus depressus* ●
   ශ්‍රී ලංකා හැලි ගේහූනා
   SVL 7-8.5cm; TL 6.5-9cm. Tail strongly depressed with sharp margin; a white band bordered by two dark lines across eye; reddish yellow with five dark brown cross-like wavy marks on body; young with five broad dark cross bands on body which are slightly narrower than interspaces, a light vertebral blotch on each; in old specimens, dark markings vague.

3. **Sri Lanka Spotted House Gecko** *Hemidactylus parvimaculatus* ●
   ශ්‍රී ලංකා පුල්ලි ගෙවල් හූනා
   SVL 5-5.5cm; TL 5-6cm. Dorsal surface of body without keeled, imbricate scales; skin rough; numerous enlarged, keeled dorsal tubercles arranged in more or less regular longitudinal series of 16-20 rows. Brownish ground colour, with three longitudinal rows of irregular dark brown spots which are smaller than the eye. A broken lateral brown band from snout to tympanum.

4. **Common House Gecko** *Hemidactylus frenatus*
   සුලබ ගේහූනා
   SVL 4.5-5.5cm; TL 5-6cm. Brownish in colour (usually uniform or sometimes with dark indistinct markings forming wavy cross bars); a brown band from nostril to above neck, bounded by darker lines, may be present or absent; tail feebly depressed with round margin.

5. **Four-claw Gecko** *Gehyra mutilata*
   චතුරන්ගුලි හූනා
   SVL 4.5-6cm; TL 55-65mm. Digits not bent at an angle but moderately to broadly dilated; terminal phalanges of all or digits II-V compressed; terminal phalanges of four outer digits free rising angularly from the dilated portion; stout body with a lateral fold; smooth tail; first inner digit well developed, broadly dialated, claw small and oftern concealed, lamellae divided.

PLATE 74

1. Common Skink *Eutropis carinata lankae*
   ගැරඩි හිකනලා / සුලබ හිකනලා
   SVL 10-12.5cm; TL 19-20cm. Brown colour. Back without any clear longitudinal dark stripes or pair of black markings. A striking light dorsolateral band present; dark labial bars or bright gular regions absent in either sex. Adpressed hind limbs reaching wrist or elbow. Largest skink in Sri Lanka.

2. Bronzegreen Little Skink *Eutropis macularia macularia*
   පිඟු හිකනලා
   SVL 5-6cm; TL 8-9cm. Dorsum without any clear longitudinal dark stripes. Pale dorsal stripe and a three-scale-wide dorsolateral stripe extends from top of postocular region across body to the length of tail; flanks often with white dots.

3. Sri Lanka Common Supple Skink *Lankascincus fallax* ●
   ශ්‍රී ලංකා සුලබ ලක්හිරළුවා
   SVL 5-5.5cm; TL 5-6cm. Light brown, with males in breeding season with white-spotted reddish throats and non-breeding males with white-spotted blackish throats.

4. Water Monitor *Varanus salvator*
   කබරගොයා
   1.8-2.2m. Nostril closer to snout tip than to eye; prominent body colour blackish with yellow markings; supraoculars larger than interorbitals.

5. Land Monitor *Varanus bengalensis*
   තලගොයා
   1.3-1.6m. Nostril midway between eye and snout tip; prominent body colour brownish with yellow markings; supraoculars smaller than interorbitals.

PLATE 75

1. Mugger Crocodile *Crocodylus paluster*
   හැල කිඹුලා
   5m. Freshwater crocodile inhabits tanks and rivers. Snout relatively broad and heavy, forehead concave, ridges in front of eyes absent. Juveniles light tan or brown with dark cross-bands on body and tail, while adults grey to brown, usually without dark bands.

2. Black Turtle *Melanochelys trijuga*
   ගල් ඉබ්බා
   38cm. Dorsal shell black. Ventral yellowish body parts. Head, legs neck visible from the outside is also blackish. One subspecies has some bright coloured spots of yellow- red on the face.

3. Sri Lanka Flapshell Turtle *Lissemys ceylonensis* 🟢
   ශ්‍රී ලංකා අළු ඉබ්බා / ශ්‍රී ලංකා කිරි ඉබ්බා
   37cm. Shell appears soft and uniform. Colour can be from blackish to yellowish green. Head with elongate long siphoniform nose.

4. Star Tortoise *Geochelone elegans*
   තාරකා ඉබ්බා / මාවර ඉබ්බා
   25cm. A star-like pattern present on both carapace and plastron. Shell dome-shaped, more elongated in adults, rounded in juveniles. Brown or black on yellow or beige, superimposed dark colour especially prominent in juveniles.

Birds
(Plate 76-106)

There is no doubt that, amongst animals on Planet Earth, birds have received the most friendly response by people. Their great appeal has encouraged an important recreational pursuit – bird watching.

Most birds are large, nearly all are diurnal, numerous, ubiquitous with many species conspicuously sharing man's environment. Their popularity and aesthetic appeal among the people come from their remarkable array of colours, behaviours and habits, especially the call or song.

Birds have evolved out of the dinosaurians (which emerged from primitive reptiles) and have many reptilian features. These are often hidden, covered by that unique bird character - feathers. Thus birds are often referred to as "glorified reptiles".

The world has over 10,000 species of birds recorded while in Sri Lanka we have recorded 495. This includes all sight records of even those that have been recorded a single time. Among them 33 species are considered endemic, of which 27 are definitive while 6 are proposed.

PLATE 76

1. **Blue Quail** *Coturnix chinensis*
   නිල් පිරිවටුවා
   15cm. **Male:** Throat and upper breast with black and white markings. Lower breast and flanks slaty blue. **Female:** Reddish-brown forehead and supercilium. Brown breast, flank with blackish bars.

2. **Barred Buttonquail** *Turnix suscitator*
   බෝලවටුවා
   16cm. Dark brown with bold black bars on buffish sides of neck, breast and wing coverts. Grey feet and bill. White eyes. **Male:** Side of head white, bold black barring on breast, orangeish buff lower flanks, thigh and undertail coverts. Throat greyish or dirty white. **Female:** Black chin, throat and center of breast. Sides of breast anterior flanks barred with black.

3. **Sri Lanka Spurfowl** *Galloperdix bicalcarata* ●
   ශ්‍රී ලංකා හබන්-කුකුළා
   33cm. Naked red orbital skin. Red legs. **Male:** Contrasting black and white spots on underparts. **Female:** Dull brownish red.

4. **Sri Lanka Junglefowl** *Gallus lafayetii* ●
   ශ්‍රී ලංකා වලි කුකුළා
   70cm. male; 35cm. female. **Male:** Crimson comb with a central yellow patch and long tail feathers. **Female:** Upperparts brown, vermiculate with black.

5. **Indian Peafowl** *Pavo cristatus*
   මොනරා
   250cm. (Male with train); 102-117cm (female and non-breeding male without train). Characteristic crest of spatula-tipped wire-like feathers. **Male:** Brilliant iridescent blue neck and breast, with long feather train. End of tail feathers with blue and gold ocelli. Feather train may be absent during the non-breeding season. Tail feathers, primaries and wing coverts reddish-brown. **Female:** Feather train absent. Head and nape reddish-brownish, rest of upper parts dull brown, faintly mottled. Lower neck metallic green. Primaries brown.

Plate 77

1. **Cotton Pygmy-goose** *Nettapus coromandelianus*
   මල්-සේරුවා
   33cm. **Male:** White head, neck and underparts, with blackish crown. Black collar. **Female:** White with diffused brown on neck and body. Dark line through eye. White supercilium.

2. **Lesser Whistling-duck** *Dendrocygna javanica*
   හීන් තඹ-සේරුවා
   40cm. Reddish–brown plumage. Sandy-brown head and neck. Dark cap and dark brown back. Upper tail coverts reddish-brown. Flank brighter brown. Sexes alike.

3. **Garganey** *Anas querquedula*
   බැමසුදු තාරාවා
   38cm. Mottled brown upperparts, white underparts. **Male:** Chocolate brown head and neck. Broad white supercilium. Small white patch at base of bill. Iridescent green speculum. **Female and NBr. Male:** Brown plumage with white patch at base of bill.

4. **Little Grebe** *Tachybaptus ruficollis*
   පුංචි ගෙඩිතුරුවා
   25cm. Small, compact, tailless appearance. Pointed bill with white patch at gape. Brown body. Wings small. When in water three-quarters of the body is above waterline. **Br:** Reddish brown throat and fore neck. **NBr:** whitish throat.

PLATE 78

1. **Painted Stork** *Mycteria leucocephala*
   ලතුවැකියා
   102cm. White plumage. Black primaries and tail. Black stripe across breast. Naked head yellowish. Bill long curved at tip and yellow. Pinkish tinge on greater wing coverts. **NBr:** Paler plumage. **Juvenile:** Blackish grey or brown plumage.

2. **Asian Openbill** *Anastomus oscitans*
   විවරතුඩුවා
   81cm. Bill with prominent gap at mid-point between mandibles. Grey white general plumage. Darker above. **NBr:** pale smoke grey and black plumage. **Juvenile:** darker.

3. **Eurasian Spoonbill** *Platalea leucorodia*
   හැඳිඅලවා
   84cm. White body plumage. Bill long and spoon shaped. **Br:** Yellowish tinge on lower neck.

4. **Black-headed Ibis** *Threskiornis melanocephalus*
   හිසකළු දැකැත්තා
   76cm. White body plumage. Beak, head and upper neck region naked and black. **Br.** Bare red patch on inner edge of under wing brightens, Black breast plumes.

5. **Lesser Adjutant** *Leptoptilos javanicus*
   හීන් බහුරු-මානාවා
   115cm. Upperparts blackish. White breast and belly. Neck head Bill Large and yellowish.

6. **Woolly-necked Stork** *Ciconia episcopus*
   පාදිලි මානාවා
   91cm. eneral body plumage, wing and crown black. Neck white feathers with "woolly" appearance. Belly white.

Plate 79

1. **Cinnamon Bittern** *Ixobrychus cinnamomeus*
   කුරුඳු මැටි-කොකා
   38cm. Slim. Uniform dark reddish-brown upperparts. Underparts duller and streaked. Prominent white chin. Bill slender. **Female:** Speckled with white on back and wing-coverts. **Juv:** Browner upper parts heavily barred.

2. **Yellow Bittern** *Ixobrychus sinensis*
   කහ මැටි-කොකා
   38cm. Slim. Yellow brown upper parts and buffy underparts. Tail and primary feathers black. **Female:** reddish-brown crown, streaked under parts. **Juv:** heavily streaked underparts.

3. **Black-crowned Night-heron** *Nycticorax nycticorax*
   රෑ-කොකා
   56cm. Black crown and back. White head plumes. Br: Reddish legs. Juv: Brown with whitish spots above and brown streaks below. Nocturnal.

4. **Indian Pond-heron** *Ardeola grayii*
   කණ-කොකා
   46cm. Ashy-brown or purplish brown, upper back. Underparts dirty white often streaked brown. Bill and legs yellow green.

5. **Black Bittern** *Ixobrychus flavicollis*
   කළු මැටි-කොකා
   58cm. Slim Blackish brown plumage. Orange brown from chin to upper breast. Sides of neck streaked with black. Bill and feet dark brown.

PLATE 80

1. **Intermediate Egret** *Mesophoyx intermedia*
   මැදි-කොකා
   71cm. **NBr:** Dark green to black legs. Pale yellow lores. **Br:** Black legs, yellow bill, green lores; plumes on upper breast and lower back.

2. **Great Egret** *Casmerodius albus*
   මහ-කොකා
   94cm. Gape extends beyond eye. **NBr:** Dark brown to black legs; yellow bill and pale greenish-yellow lores. **Br:** Black bill and green lores; plumes on lower back only. Upper tibia reddish.

3. **Cattle Egret** *Bubulcus ibis*
   ගෙරි-කොකා
   51cm. Completely white during non-breeding season. Yellow bill Legs and feet black. Puffed out prominent gular region. **Br:** Golden orange on head, neck and upper back.

4. **Little Egret** *Egretta garzetta*
   පුංචි අනු-කොකා
   61cm. Completely white plumage. Black bill and legs. Yellow-green feet. **Br:** Breeding plumes on nape, lower breast and back.

5. **Grey Heron** *Ardea cinerea*
   අළු කොකා
   94cm. Head and neck white, mantle grey. Underparts are white. Black line running to nape across eyes and occiput region. Interrupted black line down side of neck. Shoulder and outer margin of folded wing blackish.

6. **Purple Heron** *Ardea purpurea*
   කරවැල් කොකා
   79cm. General plumage reddish brown. The upper mantle has a purple sheen but appears greyish at a distance. Black crown. Long black line on the side of neck. Lores greenish. Bill and feet yellowish.

PLATE 81

1. **Spot-billed Pelican** *Pelecanus philippensis*
   තිත්හොට පැස්තුඩුවා
   140cm. Dirty white to pale greyish body. Black spots on the upper mandible. Pouch pinkish. Head has black speckles. **In flight:** Under wing has some brown.

2. **Little Cormorant** *Phalacrocorax niger*
   පුංචි දියකාවා
   51cm. Short bill. Long tail. **NBr:** Chin and upper throat white. **Br:** Small crest on forehead. **Juv:** Dark brown; chin and throat dirty white.

3. **Indian Cormorant** *Phalacrocorax fuscicollis*
   ඉන්දු දියකාවා
   65cm. Long slender bill. **NBr:** White border to gular pouch. **Br:** White feather tuft behind eye, white speckles on head and neck. **Juv:** Upper-parts dark brown. Underparts dirty white. V-formation in flight.

4. **Great Cormorant** *Phalacrocorax carbo*
   මහ දියකාවා
   91cm. Long, heavy bill. Jet black plumage. White cheeks and throat. **In flight:** Neck held slightly above horizontal. V-formation. **NBr:** Nape, hindneck and flanks black. **Juvenile:** Browner and with more white on the underparts.

5. **Oriental Darter** *Anhinga melanogaster*
   අහිකාවා
   90cm. Long slender snake-like neck and dagger-like bill. Body plumage blackish with white-streaked feathers. **Br:** More white on neck.

Plate 82

1. **Common Kestrel** *Falco tinnunculus*
   පොදු උකුසුගොයා
   34cm. **Male:** Head and nape grey. Upper back reddish brown with black spots. Breast narrowly streaked and belly spotted with black. **Female:** Upperparts reddish brown. **Immature:** Like female but heavily marked.

2. **Black-winged Kite** *Elanus caeruleus*
   කළු උරිස් පතනකුස්සා
   33cm. Pale grey upper parts. Black shoulder patch. Black eye stripe. **Immature:** Brownish tinge. May posses brown streaks on breast. **In flight:** White underparts. Black primaries. Long pointed wings.

3. **Oriental Honey-buzzard** *Pernis ptilorhyncus*
   සිළු බඹරකුස්සා
   68cm. Plumage highly variable. Upperparts brown to blackish. Head black to white. Crest usually small, tipped with white. Underparts off-white to dark brown, streaked or barred. Unevenly spaced dark tail bands in adults.

4. **Brahminy Kite** *Haliastur indus*
   බමුණු පියාකුස්සා
   45cm. Brownish red upperparts; white head and breast. **Juv:** Pale tail, dark under-wing covert.

5. **Besra** *Accipiter virgatus*
   බසරා කුරුළුගොයා
   30-35cm. Brown upper plumage. Broad, dark mesial stripe on white throat. Underparts closely barred with brown. **Male:** Upper parts blackish brown to dark slaty grey with blackish head. Breast and belly brownish grey to reddish-brown with broad white and blackish streaks in center of breast. Barred belly. **Female:** Similar to male but browner with less reddish-brown on underparts.

6. **Shikra** *Accipiter badius*
   කුරුළුගොයා
   30-35cm. **Male:** Upperparts grey brown. Cheeks tinged grey with reddish-brown. Underparts whitish with narrowly barred reddish brown on breast and belly. Tail without bands. **Female:** Larger, browner upperparts. Throat greyish. Under surface lacks reddish brown barring. Central tail feather has a distinct sub-terminal band.

PLATE 83

1. Grey-headed Fish-eagle *Ichthyophaga ichthyaetus*
   අඵහිස් මසුකුස්සා
   71cm. Upperparts dark brown. Head and throat grey. Breast brown. Lower belly, undertail coverts and basal two-thirds of tail white. **Juvenile:** Similar to adults but upperparts paler. Whitish-brown eyebrow. Underparts pale brown streaked with white. **In flight:** Underparts contrast sharply with white of lower belly and tail base.

2. White-bellied Sea-eagle *Haliaeetus leucogaster*
   කුසඇලි මුහුදුකුස්සා
   73cm. White head, underparts, neck and third of tail. Rest ashy grey. **Juvenile:** Brownish. **In flight:** Wings broad at base, held strongly forward and raised in a shallow "V". Short wedge-shaped tail. Wing lining white. Primaries and secondaries black.

3. Changeable Hawk-eagle *Spizaetus cirrhatus*
   පෙරළි කොණ්ඩකුස්සා
   69cm. Dark-tipped feathers form distinct vertical crest. Plumage colour varies considerably. Upper parts vary from pale to dark brown to almost white. Underparts from dark brown streaks to almost buffy brown to white. **In flight:** Undersides whitish with black bands. Tail banded.

4. Crested Serpent Eagle *Spilornis cheela*
   සිළු සරපකුස්සා
   51-71cm. Dark brown plumage, spotted with yellow above and white below. Small crest often lying flat on the head giving a characteristic shape to the crown. Yellow feet, base of bill and eyes. Tail with broad white band. **In flight:** Broad white band along the length of the wing separates black tips of flight feathers from rest of the wing.

PLATE 84

1. **White-breasted Waterhen** *Amaurornis phoenicurus*
   ළයසුදු කොරවක්කා
   33cm. White breast, throat and face. Under tail reddish brown. Twitching upturned tail. **Immature:** Completely black.

2. **Purple Swamphen** *Porphyrio porphyrio*
   දම් මැදි-කිතලා
   43cm. Purplish blue body; large red bill and red frontal shield. Long red legs. **Juv:** Dull in colour.

3. **Common Coot** *Fulica atra*
   පොදු කිතලා
   38cm. Black plumage. White bill and frontal shield. Narrow white trailing edge to wing. Legs green.

4. **Common Moorhen** *Gallinula chloropus*
   පොදු ගැලිනුවා
   33cm. Back slaty grey with dark brown. Bill red with yellow tip. Headshield red. Undertail coverts white divided in two by black vertical partition. A clear white line on sides of flank.

5. **Eurasian Thick-knee** *Burhinus oedicnemus*
   ගොළු-කිරළා
   40cm. Greenish brown body. Short black and yellow bill. Long yellowish legs. Black and white bars across wing coverts. White band across the face.

6. **Great Thick-knee** *Esacus recurvirostris*
   මාගොළු-කිරළා
   50cm. Sandy brown body. Slightly upcurved, heavy, black and yellow bill. White forehead with spectacles. Black line on shoulder.

7. **Black-winged Stilt** *Himantopus himantopus*
   කළුපිය ඉපල්පාවා
   38cm. Long red legs, thin long black bill. Hindneck is usually white or grey, sometimes blackish. Head often sullied with grey. Black and white body. **Juv. and female:** Brownish upperparts.

PLATE 85

1. **Yellow-wattled Lapwing** *Vanellus malabaricus*
   කහ යටිමල් කිරළා
   28cm. Yellow wattles, long yellow legs. Black cap and white band through eye. Sandy brown upperparts and white belly.

2. **Red-wattled Lapwing** *Vanellus indicus*
   රත් යටිමල් කිරළා
   30cm. Red bill with black tip. Red wattle and irides, long yellow legs. White cheeks. Black head, neck and upper breast. Distinctive call: 'Did-he-do-it'.

3. **Pacific Golden Plover** *Pluvialis fulva*
   සෙත්කර රන් මහ-ඕලෙවියා
   25cm. Golden yellow and black mottled upperparts. Yellowish buff supercillium, neck and cheek. **Br:** Face, neck breast and abdomen black.

4. **Little Ringed Plover** *Charadrius dubius*
   පුංචි මාල ඕලෙවියා
   16cm. Upper breast and upper back encircled by a black band. Eye ring, legs, and sometimes base of lower mandible, yellow.

5. **Kentish Plover** *Charadrius alexandrinus*
   කෙන්ටි ඕලෙවියා
   18cm. General plumage like Little Ringed Plover. No black band on upper back. Incomplete breast-bands confined to patches on sides of breast. The black mask is restricted to a bar across the eye and a small patch on the forecrown. Black bill. Dark grey legs. **Female:** Head and breast markings paler.

6. **Lesser Sand Plover** *Charadrius mongolus*
   හීන් වැලි ඕලෙවියා
   20cm. Short, slimmer and less pointed bill. Head more rounded than Kentish Plover. Dark brown or dark grey legs. Taller than Kentish Plover.

PLATE 86

1. **Pheasant-tailed Jacana** *Hydrophasianus chirurgus*
   සැවුල් දියසෑනා
   30cm. (breeding 50cm). White head and foreneck, yellowish hindneck. White wing and dark brown body. Long curved tail and brown underparts in breeding season.

2. **Pintail Snipe** *Gallinago stenura*
   උල්පෙඳ කැස්වටුවා
   25cm. Dark brown upperparts highly marked by black, rufous, buff scales. White belly. Blunt tipped long bill. Prominent mantle and scapular stripes.

3. **Marsh Sandpiper** *Tringa stagnatilis*
   වගුරු සිලිබිල්ලා
   25cm. Slim, whitish plumage, greyish brown above. Forehead, supercillium, sides of head and rump pure white. Underparts pure white. Breast may be marked faintly with brown. Tail narrowly barred. Bill thin and long. Legs long.

4. **Common Redshank** *Tringa totanus*
   පොදු රන්පා සිලිබිල්ලා
   28cm. Uniformly greyish plumage. Bill black with red base. Legs orange-red. White rump. Underparts white. **In flight:** Broad white bar on trailing edge of wing.

5. **Wood Sandpiper** *Tringa glareola*
   වන සිලිබිල්ලා
   23cm. Greyish-brown and indistinctly spotted and marked with white. Whitish supercilium. Underparts white with pale dusky breast. Lower back, rump and tail white. Tail barred with black. Legs yellowish. Supercilium extends beyond eye. Legs greenish-yellow.

6. **Common Greenshank** *Tringa nebularia*
   පොදු පලාපා සිලිබිල්ලා
   35cm. Dark greyish brown. White forehead, lower back. Tail and rump barred. Underparts white. Bill large and slightly upturned at the tip.

7. **Common Sandpiper** *Actitis hypoleucos*
   පොදු සිලින්තා
   20cm. Plain brown upper surface. White underparts. Brown breast-patch. Bobs its tail continuously. Short black legs. **In flight:** Broad white wing bar, white outer tail feathers and dark rump. Characteristic flight with shallow flicking of bowed wings.

PLATE 87

1. Gull-billed Tern *Sterna nilotica*
   ගලතුඩු මුහුදුලිහිණියා
   38cm. Pale ashy-grey back and wings. Short stout black bill. Head whitish (may posses dark streaks) with small blackish patch behind eye. Stout body and fairly broad wings. Appears white when in flight. **Summer plumage:** Black cap. **Breeding:** Breeds on islets off north-west coast..

2. Roseate Tern *Sterna dougallii*
   අරුණූ මුහුදුලිහිණියා
   33cm. Pale grey plumage. Tail deeply forked with outer feathers white. Black bill and legs. Tail project well beyond folded wing. **Br:** Pinkish tinge on underparts. Black cap. Bill black with red base, or completely red.

3. Common Tern *Sterna hirundo*
   පොදු මුහුදුලිහිණියා
   33cm. Grey and white plumage. Tail deeply forked. Outer tail feathers long. Outer edge of tail often blackish. Nape black. Leading edge of inner half of wing-lining blackish. Bill black. Feet dusky red to black. At rest tip of tail extends slightly beyond end of folded wing. Whitish rump. **Br:** Black cap.

4. Little Tern *Sterna albifrons*
   පුංචි මුහුදුලිහිණියා
   23cm. Plumage greyish-white. Head with black cap often suffused with white. Black bill, legs dusky-red. **Summer:** Black cap. Forehead white. Orange bill and legs. **In flight:** 2-3 outer primaries black. Pale greyish upperparts and wings contrasting with white rump. Rapid wing beats; wing action "high" ie, in flight the wings do not descend much below the body line.

5. Whiskered Tern *Chlidonias hybrida*
   අළුපිය කාගුල්ලිහිණියා
   28cm. **NBr:** Black cap extending on to rear crown and hind neck, but not below eye, streaky appearance in the region of the forehead. **Br:** Black belly.

PLATE 88

1. **Rock Pigeon** *Columba livia*
   පරෙවියා
   33cm. Blue-grey. The rump area is grey in the wild variety and whiter in the domestic variety. Two broad black bars on wing. Black bar at tip of tail. Whitish underwing. Neck darker, glossed with green and purplish-blue. Black bill. Red feet.

2. **Spotted Dove** *Stigmatopelia chinensis*
   අළු-කොබෙයියා
   30cm. Blue grey with a pinkish brown tinge. Spotted with white above. A black and white "checker board" pattern on hindneck. Long white-tipped tail. Pinkish grey throat. White belly, vent and tail coverts. Bill brown to black. Feet red.

3. **Emerald Dove** *Chalcophaps indica*
   නීල-කොබෙයියා
   25cm. Bronze metallic green above. Crown and neck grey tinged with blue. Rest of body dark reddish brown. White forehead and eye brow. Two white bands across lower back. Whitish margin at bend of wing. Bill red, feet purplish red. **Female:** Duller than male. Blue-grey crown and upper neck. Lateral tail feathers rufous. **Habits:** Flies rapidly turning from side to side to avoid obstacles.

4. **Orange-breasted Green-pigeon** *Treron bicinctus*
   ළයරන් බටගොයා
   25cm. Yellowish-green plumage. Hindneck, nape and upper tail grey. Pale underparts. **Male:** Bright orange breast with purplish breast band. Undertail pale reddish-brown. **Female:** Paler breast, vent and tail coverts. Central tail feathers bluish.

5. **Pompadour Green-pigeon** *Treron pompadora* ●
   රන්බොර බටගොයා
   25cm. Dark yellowish-green plumage paler underparts. Yellow wing bar. Ashy blue crown and nape. **Male:** Maroon back. **Female:** Greenish back. Middle tail feathers yellowish-green. Undertail coverts yellowish mottled with white with greyish-green.

6. **Green Imperial-pigeon** *Ducula aenea*
   නිල් මහගොයා
   43cm. Metallic green with bronze sheen. Head, neck, and underparts grey with pinkish tinge. Undertail coverts brownish. Red eyes and feet.

PLATE 89

1. **Sri Lanka Hanging-parrot** *Loriculus beryllinus* ●
   ශ්‍රී ලංකා ගිරාමලිත්තා
   14cm. Grass-green plumage. Small short square tail. Red crown and rump. Orange nape, yellowish tinge on hindneck and upper back. **Male:** Small blue patch on throat. **Female:** Similar but duller and shows only traces of blue throat patch.

2. **Rose-ringed Parakeet** *Psittacula krameri*
   රෑන ගිරවා
   40cm. Green plumage. Long tail. Red hooked bill, with lower mandible blackish. Feet dark greenish. Male-rose pink hindneck collar continues as black band in front of throat. Female lacks collar but with indistinct emerald green ring around neck.

3. **Alexandrine Parakeet** *Psittacula eupatria*
   ලබු ගිරවා
   51cm. Green plumage. Large red hooked bill. Red patch on secondary wing coverts. Feet yellowish. Long tail. Male has rose-pink collar around most of neck, but black where it meets lower mandible. **Female:** Lacks collar and black mandibular region. Green throat.

4. **Plum-headed Parakeet** *Psittacula cyanocephala*
   පඩු ගිරවා
   34cm. Slender bird. Green tinged yellow plumage. Broad white tips to bluish central long tail feathers. **Male:** Rose-pink head with violet-blue tinge on crown and nape. Black throat and narrow collar around neck. Red patch on shoulder. Bill orange-yellow to orange. **Female:** Dull grey-violet head with yellow collar. No shoulder patch.

PLATE 90

1. **Chestnut-winged Cuckoo** *Clamator coromandus*
   තඹල පිය කොණ්ඩකොහා
   5cm. Distinct black crest. Long tail. Black upperparts with white nuchal collar. Reddish-brown wings. Rust coloured chin, throat and upper breast. Rest of underparts white or whitish. Black bill and legs.

2. **Pied Cuckoo** *Clamator jacobinus*
   ගෝමර කොණ්ඩකොහා
   35cm. Crested. Long-tailed black and white bird. Entire upperparts black, with white patch on wing. Underparts white and tail feathers tipped with white.

3. **Indian Cuckoo** *Cuculus micropterus*
   ඉන්දු කෝකිලයා
   33cm. Dark slaty-grey above with a brownish tinge. Underparts pale ash-grey and white with black crossbars. Dull greyish green eye ring. Broad black sub-terminal band on tail. Distinct call during the months of February to about early June.

4. **Banded Bay Cuckoo** *Cacomantis sonneratii*
   වයිර අනුකොහා
   23cm. Upperparts bright brownish-red with dark brown crossbars. Pale supercillium. Underparts whitish with brown barring. Tail brownish-red, tipped with white.

5. **Grey-bellied Cuckoo** *Cacomantis passerinus*
   කුසළු අනුකොහා
   21cm. Grey head, throat and upper breast. Pale on abdomen, whitish on vent. Tail blackish with a white tip and outer tail feathers obliquely barred white. White patch on underside of wing seen during flight. "Hepatic" female has bright reddish-brown upperparts and throat. Cross-barred with black on back. Finely black barred white underparts. Lacks the whitish supercilium of previous species. Sides of head are buff, distinguishing it from the Banded Bay Cuckoo. The female grey phase resembles the male.

6. **Drongo Cuckoo** *Surniculus lugubris*
   කවුඩුකොහා
   23cm. Entirely black with slightly forked tail. White bars on undertail coverts and outer tail feathers. Its feeding behaviour and thin bill distinguish it from drongos.

PLATE 91

1. **Asian Koel** *Eudynamys scolopaceus*
   කොවුලා
   43cm. Red irides. **Male:** Glossy black plumage. **Female:** Brown, profusely spotted and barred with white. Parasitizes both species of crows. Highly vocal, from March–June.

2. **Sri Lanka Red-faced Malkoha** *Phaenicophaeus pyrrhocephalus* 🟢
   ශ්‍රී ලංකා වතරතු මල්කොහා
   45cm. Blackish with blue-green sheen above. Speckled with white on nape. Naked bright red patch around eye which extends to the apple-green bill. Tail long, graduated greenish-black with white tips. White belly. **Male:** Irides brown. **Female:** Irides white.

3. **Blue-faced Malkoha** *Phaenicophaeus viridirostris*
   වතනිල් මල්කොහා
   39cm. Grey-black above, with long graduated tail tipped with white. Underparts pale grey-white. Face has a bare blue eye-ring. Bill apple-green.

4. **Sirkeer Malkoha** *Phaenicophaeus leschenaultii*
   පතන් මල්කොහා (පතන් ඇටිකුකුළා)
   43cm. Sandy brown plumage. Long tail with white tipped lateral tail-feathers. Bright red to yellow–red bill. Black streaks on head and breast feathers.

5. **Greater Coucal** *Centropus sinensis*
   ඇටි-කුකුළා
   48cm. Completely black body with reddish brown wings. Tail graduated and long. Red eyes. Bill black and slightly hooked.

PLATE 92

1. **Collared Scops-owl** *Otus bakkamoena*
   කරපටි කන්බස්සා
   23cm. Upperparts dull buffish brown or greyish-brown plumage with bright buff neck collar. Underparts white to rich buff streaked with black, and with fine wavy bars of reddish-brown. Throat also barred. Chin plain. Irides brown. Bill blackish grey.

2. **Spot-bellied Eagle-owl** *Bubo nipalensis*
   උකුසුබකමුණා (උලමා)
   61cm. A large species. Eartufts black and white. Upperparts dark brown with buff scaly marks. Underparts buffish-white with blackish bars on throat, breast and spots on belly. Irides brown.

3. **Brown Fish-owl** *Ketupa zeylonensis*
   බොර කෙවුල්බකමුණා
   54cm. Small eartufts. Legs naked. Upperparts dark brown heavily streaked with black. Underparts whitish with fine bars of black and brown. White patch on throat and foreneck. Eyes yellow.

4. **Jungle Owlet** *Glaucidium radiatum*
   වන උපබස්සා
   20cm. Upperparts dark brown closely barred with brownish-buff. Underparts, chin, moustachial streak, middle of breast and abdomen white. Rest barred dark yellowish-green, brown and white.

5. **Indian Nightjar** *Caprimulgus asiaticus*
   ඉන්දු බිම්බස්සා
   23cm. andy brown plumage with black and buff markings. Small white patch on either side of throat. Black streaks on back.

6. **Jerdon's Nightjar** *Caprimulgus atripennis*
   දිගුපෙඳ බිම්බස්සා
   30cm. Large. Contrastingly marked and relatively long-tailed. **Male:** Prominent white patches on outer two tail feathers. Throat whitish. **Female:** White patch on primaries.

PLATE 93

1. **Indian Swiftlet** *Aerodramus unicolor*
   ඉන්දු උප-තුරිතයා
   13cm. Slender with blackish brown upperparts. Rump blackish. Underparts brown. Tail notched (slightly forked).

2. **Asian Palm-swift** *Cypsiurus balasiensis*
   ආසියා තල්-තුරිතයා
   13cm. Slender. Dark brown above and below. Slightly lighter towards abdomen. Narrow thin, deeply forked tail.

3. **Little Swift** *Apus affinis*
   පුංචි තුරිතයා
   15cm. Completely black with prominent white rump. Tail slightly forked.

4. **Barn Swallow** *Hirundo rustica*
   අටු වැහිළිහිණියා
   15cm. Glossy dark blue above; blackish blue breast band. Bright reddish brown forehead and throat. Underparts dirty white to light brownish. Deeply forked tail.

5. **Crested Treeswift** *Hemiprocne coronata*
   සිළු රුක්-තුරිතයා
   23cm. Blue-grey above. Crest on forehead and deeply forked tail. **Male:** Sides of face reddish brown.

6. **Red-rumped Swallow** *Hirundo daurica* ●
   නිතඹ රත් වැහිළිහිණියා
   18cm. Dark metallic blue above. Rump reddish brown. Underparts range from reddish brown to white with heavy streaking on breast and flanks. Open country. Frequently in small groups, commoner at mid-elevations.

PLATE 94

1. Malabar Trogon *Harpactes fasciatus*
   ලෝහවන්නිච්චා
   30cm. **Male:** White necklace separating black breast from brilliant red underparts. **Female:** Underparts yellowish brown.

2. Indian Roller *Coracias benghalensis*
   දුම්බොන්නා
   33cm. Brownish–red back and breast. Pale blue abdomen, vent and crown. Blue wing and tail with dark edge at bend of wing. Base of primaries dark. Base of tail, tip of tail and collar around hindneck reddish-brown.

3. Blue-tailed Bee-eater *Merops philippinus*
   නිල්පෙද බිඟුහරයා
   30cm. Dull green head and nape. Bluish lower back, rump and tail. Black line through eye to bill. Yellow chin, throat is reddish-brown. Underparts light green. Central tail feathers elongated. Insects pursued and caught in flight.

4. Little Green Bee-eater *Merops orientalis*
   පුංචි බිඟුහරයා
   20cm. Grass-green plumage. Reddish-brown head. Hindneck, chin and throat sea blue bordered below by a black line. Black line through eye. Elongated thin central tail feathers.

5. Chestnut-headed Bee-eater *Merops leschenaulti*
   තඹල හිස් බිඟුහරයා
   17cm. Grass-green plumage. Crown, hindneck and upper back bright reddish-brown. Chin and throat yellow, bordered by black. Rump and lower back bright blue. Bill black. Lacks elongated central tail-feathers.

6. Eurasian Hoopoe *Upupa epops*
   පොරෝඋවා
   30cm. Reddish-brown plumage. Black wings with broad white bands. Tail black with a single white band in the middle. Prominent brown crest with black tips. Crest is often retracted. Long curved bill.

Plate 95

1. **Stork-billed Kingfisher** *Pelargopsis capensis*
   මානාතුඩු මහ-පිළිහුඩුවා
   38cm. Dull blue upperparts. Bright blue rump. Brown head. Orange collar and neck. Underparts brownish yellow. Chin and throat whitish. Large red bill.

2. **Black-capped Kingfisher** *Halcyon pileata*
   කළු ඉසැසි මැදි-පිළිහුඩුවා
   30cm. Purple-blue above (appears black in some lighting conditions). Black head. White collar on hindneck. Underparts light brown. Dark red bill.

3. **White-throated Kingfisher** *Halcyon smyrnensis*
   ගෙලසුදු මැදි-පිළිහුඩුවා
   28cm. Iridescent blue back. Chocolate brown head, sides of breast and belly. White chin, throat and breast. Dull red bill and feet.

4. **Black-backed Kingfisher** *Ceyx erithaca*
   පෙරදිගු හීන්-පිළිහුඩුවා
   13cm. Orange-violet on the back. Wings dark purple-blue. Rest of upperparts orange. Underparts bright yellow-pink. Blue patch on forehead and behind ear coverts. Bill and feet orange-red.

5. **Pied Kingfisher** *Ceryle rudis*
   ගෝමර-පිළිහුඩුවා
   30cm. Black and white plumage. White breast with horizontal black bars. Bill and feet black. **Male:** Two complete black breast bands. **Female:** Only one band present; this is frequently broken in the centre.

6. **Common Kingfisher** *Alcedo atthis*
   මල් පිළිහුඩුවා
   18cm. Blue back and rump. Wings are dark blue with bars. Bright orange-brown underparts. Reddish-brown cheeks, ear coverts, side of neck, area behind ear coverts and chin. Short black tail.

PLATE 96

1. **Malabar Pied Hornbil** *Anthracoceros coronatus*
පෝරු කැදැත්තා
61cm. Large casque. **Male:** Has black on rear of casque and red eye. **Female:** White facial skin and brown irides. Posterior edge of casque black. Roosts in large numbers during the non-breeding season.

2. **Sri Lanka Grey Hornbil** *Ocyceros gingalensis* ●
ශ්‍රී ලංකා අළු-කැදැත්තා
59cm. Grey upper-plumage with a slight tinge of brown to black. White underparts. Dark long tail tipped white. Curved bill very large and long: cream in male. **Female:** Bill dull black with a longitudinal cream patch on sides of the upper mandible.

3. **Brown-headed Barbet** *Megalaima zeylanica*
පොලොස් කොට්ටෝරුවා
26cm. Grass-green plumage with white streaks. Brown head, breast and upper back. Bare orange patch around eye extends to base of bill. Undersurface of tail bluish. Bill large and orangish brown. Feet yellow. Whiskers at base of bill.

4. **Coppersmith Barbet** *Megalaima haemacephala*
රත්ළය කොට්ටෝරුවා
15cm. Grass-green plumage. Red forehead and large red breast patch. Yellow throat, yellow above and below eye. Underparts pale yellowish-green with broad streaks. Bill and feet black.

5. **Crimson-fronted Barbet** *Megalaima rubricapillus*
රත් මුණත් කොට්ටෝරුවා
14cm. Grass-green plumage. Red forehead and small breast patch. Chin, throat supecilium and area just below the eye orange-yellow. Blue on side of neck. Underparts light green. Bill and feet black.

6. **Indian Pitta** *Pitta brachyura*
අවිච්චියා
19cm. Upper back greenish becoming bluish towards rump, uppertail coverts and tail. Blue patch on shoulder. Central crown, nape, sides of face down to base of neck. White supercilium separates the black region of the face from the brown streak above it. Small white crescent below eye. Chin, throat and side of lower neck are white. Underparts orangish brown with belly and vent reddish. Bill black.

PLATE 97

1. **Brown-capped Woodpecker** *Dendrocopos nanus*
   බොර ඉසැසි පිරි-කැරලා
   13cm. Upperparts dark brown (almost black) with white markings. Underparts white with very pale streaks. Sometimes clear white line from above eye extending down the side of neck. **Male:** Red-streak on occipital region.

2. **Yellow-crowned Woodpecker** *Dendrocopos mahrattensis*
   කහසිඑු පිරි-කැරලා
   19cm. Head with small crest. Forehead and crown brownish–yellow. Brownish-black above with irregular white marking on back and wings. Underparts chin, throat and foreneck white, rest creamy white with dark brown streaks. Red abdominal patch. **Male:** Occipital region red and nape black. **Female:** Occipital red of male replaced with brown.

3. **Lesser Yellownape** *Picus chlorolophus*
   හීන් කහ ගෙලැසි කැරලා
   20cm. Yellowish-green plumage. Yellow nape. Tail brownish black. Chin and throat brown, barred with white. White streaks on sides of belly and undertail coverts. **Male:** Red forehead, crest and head. Red moustachial streak. **Female:** Forepart of head grey, less red. No moustachial streak.

4. **Rufous Woodpecker** *Celeus brachyurus*
   බොරන් අනු-කැරලා
   25cm. Body oval-shaped. Brown with a reddish tinge to plumage. Small narrow black bars on upperparts. Underparts with much narrower barring, almost uniform brown. Black bill no crest. Longish flattened forehead.

5. **Black-rumped Flameback** *Dinopium benghalense*
   ගිනිපිට පිලි-කැරලා
   28cm. Head with crest. Red above. Underparts white streaked with black. Black chin and throat. Sides of head black with white markings. A prominent white streak which starts at base of the bill continues below the eye to the shoulder. Another white streak from above eye extends almost to the nape. **Male:** Red crest. **Female:** Forehead black with white streaks. Crest black with small elongated white spots.

6. **Greater Flameback** *Chrysocolaptes lucidus* ●
   ලේපිට මහ-කැරලා
   33cm. Head with crimson crest. Crimson back. Upper tailcoverts and tail black. Underparts with black and white scale-like pattern. Cheeks and chin with white and black stripes running down face. Two black stripes commencing at base of bill separated by a white island meet as a single stripe which descends down the neck and continues to the shoulder area. The island thus formed is a diagnostic field characteristic. Bill is paler at the tip. **Male:** Red crown and crest. **Female:** White-spotted black crest.

PLATE 98

1. **Ashy Woodswallow** *Artamus fuscus*
   අළු වනලිහිණියා
   18cm. Grey plumage, darker around eyes. Bill wide, light blue. Long folded wing and square tail. Flight very swallow-like.

2. **Common Iora** *Aegithina tiphia*
   පොදු අයෝරාවා
   15cm. Yellowish underparts. Two white bars on wings. **Male:** Black above. **Female:** Greenish-yellow above.

3. **Common Woodshrike** *Tephrodornis pondicerianus* 🟠
   පොදු වනසැරටිත්තා
   14cm. Grey-brown upper plumage. Short tail. Dark grey mask. Supercilium and outer tail feathers white. Underparts dirty white. Pale grey rump. Black bill and legs. Female browner.

4. **Large Cuckooshrike** *Coracina macei*
   මහ කොවුල්සැරටිත්තා
   30cm. Upper plumage grey. Underparts whitish. Black mask. Bill and feet black. **Male:** Plain breast area. **Female:** Body paler. Mask less pronounced. Dark grey bars on throat and breast.

5. **Black-headed Cuckooshrike** *Coracina melanoptera*
   කළුහිස් කොවුල්සැරටිත්තා
   19cm. **Male:** Black head, white belly and vent. **Female:** Upperparts grey-brown and barred.

6. **Small Minivet** *Pericrocotus cinnamomeus*
   පුංචි මිණිවිත්තා
   16cm. **Male:** Bright yellowish red breast and belly. **Female:** Dusky white throat, tinged with yellow on the breast. Often in small flocks.

7. **Scarlet Minivet** *Pericrocotus flammeus*
   දිලිරත් මිණිවිත්තා
   20cm. **Male:** Bright scarlet and black plumage. **Female:** Yellow, grey and black plumage. Often in small flocks.

8. **Brown Shrike** *Lanius cristatus*
   බොර සබරිත්තා
   19cm. Heavy, black, hooked beak. Head relatively large. Uniform grey-brown to reddish brown upperparts. Adults darker than juveniles. White forehead and eyebrow. Black mask. Underparts buff to white.

PLATE 99

1. Black-hooded Oriole *Oriolus xanthornus*
   කහකුරුල්ලා
   25cm. Black hood. Brilliant yellow with black plumage. **Juv:** Duller with streaked throat.

2. White-bellied Drongo *Dicrurus caerulescens*
   කවුඩා
   24cm. White from belly to vent and glossy blue-black plumage.

3. Greater Racket-tailed Drongo *Dicrurus paradiseus*
   පිතිපෙඳ කවුඩා
   30-35cm. Plumage glossy black. Prominent crest on forehead. Tail varies from racket-shaped outer feather to elongated folded feathers. The racket tail is present only among some individuals of the dry zone race.

4. Asian Paradise-flycatcher *Terpsiphone paradisi*
   රැහැන්මාරා
   20cm. (40cm. with tail streamer). Two subspecies:
   (i) *T. p. ceylonensis* -Brown or dark phase.
   Both male and female brown. Male has long tail.
   (ii) *T. p. paradisi* - Indian or white phase. The male is either white or brown. Female always brown.
   Males have long tails.

5. Black-naped Monarch *Hypothymis azurea*
   කළු ගෙලැසි රදමාරා
   15cm. Blue with black nape. **Female:** Duller and more brown than male.

6. White-browed Fantail *Rhipidura aureola*
   බැමසුදු පවන්පෙන්දා
   16cm. White eye brow, spots on wing. "Dancing" habit.

PLATE 100

1. **Jungle Crow** *Corvus levaillantii*
   කළු කපුටා
   48cm. Glossy black plumage. Large heavy bill is larger than in next species.

2. **House Crow** *Corvus splendens*
   කොළඹ කපුටා
   40cm. Completely black with grey collar and upper breast.

3. **Great Tit** *Parus cinereus*
   මහ ටිකිරිත්තා
   13cm. Black head, white cheek; black throat and upper breast.

4. **Jerdon's Bushlark** *Mirafra affinis*
   පඳුරු ගොමරිට්ටා
   15cm. Upperparts streaked with blackish brown. Underparts buffish with dark streaks on breast. Hindneck paler. Stout build.

5. **Oriental Skylark** *Alauda gulgula*
   පෙරදිගු අහස්රිට්ටා
   16cm. Similar to Jerdon's Bushlark but greyer and slightly smaller. Longer tail. Upperparts brown with dark streaks. Underparts brownish buff with streaks on breast. Wing is greyer (not brownish-red as in Jerdon's Bushlark). White outer tail-feathers. Nape area greyish.

6. **Ashy-crowned Sparrow Lark** *Eremopterix griseus*
   කිරුළළු බිම්රිට්ටා
   13cm. Sparrow-like. **Male:** Pale grey to sandy-brown plumage. Brownish-black chin, breast, abdomen and line through the eye. Brown cap, white cheeks and side of breast. Black bill. **Female:** Very much like female House Sparrow, but greyer.

7. **Oriental White-eye** *Zosterops palpebrosus*
   පෙරදිගු සිතැසියා
   10cm. White eye ring with a small gap in the anterior region. Greenish yellow upperparts with fine, narrow bill.

8. **Velvet-fronted Nuthatch** *Sitta frontalis*
   විල්ලුද යටිකුරිත්තා
   13cm. Red bill, velvet black forehead, lavender blue above and white throat.

Plate 101

1. **Zitting Cisticola** *Cisticola juncidis*
   ඉටි පවන්සැරියා
   13cm. Short tail with white tips. Buff supercilium and dark streaks on head, mantle and scapulars.

2. **Grey-breasted Prinia** *Prinia hodgsonii*
   ළයළු ප්‍රිණියා
   12cm. Breast with a grey band, complete in the male and interrupted in the female; ashy grey upperparts.

3. **Jungle Prinia** *Prinia sylvatica*
   වන ප්‍රිණියා
   15cm. Broad bill; darker plumage; short, buff supercilium not extending beyond eye.

4. **Ashy Prinia** *Prinia socialis*
   අළු ප්‍රිණියා
   12cm. Lack of grey breast band. Underparts orange-brown; ashy grey upperparts.

5. **Plain Prinia** *Prinia inornata*
   සරල ප්‍රිණියා
   14cm. White eye brow and darker eye stripe. Dull brown upperparts and pale buff underparts. Distinct supercilium.

6. **Common Tailorbird** *Orthotomus sutorius*
   බට්ටිච්චා
   13cm. Long usually erected tail. Reddish-brown crown. Male has extended central tail feathers.

7. **Blyth's Reed-warbler** *Acrocephalus dumetorum*
   බලයි පන්රුවියා
   14cm. Olive brown plumage with small supercilium. Longish bill with pink base. Chirps when foraging.

8. **Large-billed Leaf-warbler** *Phylloscopus magnirostris*
   මාතුඩු ගස්රුවියා
   12cm. Greenish brown plumage. Darker crown. Prominent yellowish supercilium. Feeds among leaves. Regular call like the "squeak of a swing".

PLATE 102

1. Black-crested Bulbul *Pycnonotus melanicterus*
   කළු ඉසැසි කොණ්ඩයා
   19cm. Black head, olive green upperparts; yellow throat and underparts.

2. White-browed Bulbul *Pycnonotus luteolus*
   බැමසුදු කොණ්ඩයා
   20cm. White supercilium. Brown crown with olive green upperparts and white underparts. A noisy bird with a rolling call.

3. Red-vented Bulbul *Pycnonotus cafer*
   කොණ්ඩයා
   20cm. Black head with crest. Red vent and white rump.

4. Asian Black Bulbul *Hypsipetes leucocephalus*
   කළු පිරි-කොණ්ඩයා
   23cm. Red bill and legs. Glossy black head with tufted crest and slightly forked tail.

5. Brahminy Starling *Sturnus pagodarum*
   බමුණු සැරිකාවා
   21cm. Black crown. Reddish brown upper plumage, lighter below. Grey/black on wings. Bill and legs yellowish.

6. Common Myna *Acridotheres tristis*
   මයිනා
   23cm. Brownish plumage with yellow orbital skin.

7. Rosy Starling *Sturnus roseus*
   රෝස සැරිකාවා
   23cm. Rose and black plumage. **NBr:** Head and neck dull slaty grey with buff fringes. Large aggregates.

8. Hill Myna *Gracula religiosa*
   සැලලිහිණියා
   25cm. Large orange to yellow bill. Pair of yellow wattles on nape.

Plate 103

1. **Sri Lanka Brown-capped Babbler** *Pellorneum fuscocapillus* 🟢
   ශ්‍රී ලංකා බොරග පිරි-දෙමලිච්චා
   15cm. Dark brown to blackish cap. Brown upperparts; supercilium, face and underparts are lighter.

2. **Tawny-bellied Babbler** *Dumetia hyperythra*
   කුසකහ ලදු-දෙමලිච්චා
   13cm. Olive brown above. Reddish-brown cap. White chin, throat center of breast and around eye. Rust-coloured belly. Breast edged with yellow.

3. **Sri Lanka Scimitar-babbler** *Pomatorhinus melanurus* 🟢
   ශ්‍රී ලංකා දෑ-දෙමලිච්චා
   22cm. Blackish-brown above. White below. White eyebrow. Long sickle shaped yellow bill. Call distinct duet, where the male call is followed by that of the female. **Habits:** In WZ frequently associated with mixed feeding flocks. In DZ prefers dense forests with high humidity.

4. **Dark-fronted Babbler** *Rhopocichla atriceps*
   වතඳුරු පළරු-දෙමලිච්චා
   10cm. Dark brown above. White underparts. Black forehead and around eye.

5. **Yellow-eyed Babbler** *Chrysomma sinense*
   නෙත්කහ තණ-දෙමලිච්චා
   18cm. Upper parts greyish brown. Underparts, supercilium, and lores whitish. Forehead dark brown. Orange yellow eye-ring. Long tail.

6. **Yellow-billed Babbler** *Turdoides affinis*
   දෙමලිච්චා
   23cm. Entire plumage sandy grey-brown. Lighter underparts. Pale yellow bill and legs. Pale orbital region, eyes bluish and anemic-looking.

PLATE 104

1. Oriental Magpie Robin *Copsychus saularis*
   පොල්කිච්චා
   20cm. Black and white plumage. Glossy black head, back, throat, upper breast, center tail feathers and primaries. Abdomen, wing marking and outer tail feathers white. **Female:** Duller and greyer.

2. Indian Robin *Saxicoloides fulicatus*
   කළුකිච්චා
   16cm. **Male:** Glossy blue-black. White wing patch visible in flight. **Female:** Brownish, without white wing patch.

3. White-rumped Shama *Copsychus malabaricus*
   වන පොල්කිච්චා
   25cm. **Male:** Glossy black head, breast, back and tail. White rump. Lower breast and belly reddish-brown. Long tail with outer feathers white. Legs and bill black.

4. Asian Brown Flycatcher *Muscicapa daurica*
   බොර මැසිමාරා
   13cm. Ashy-brown above. Whitish underparts. Breast and flanks greyish-brown. Large eye with white eye ring. Pale edges to wing. Bill black. Lower mandible base yellow. Black feet.

5. Brown-breasted Flycatcher *Muscicapa muttui*
   ළයබොර මැසිමාරා
   14cm. Dark ashy-brown above. Breast and flanks brown to buffish-brown. Belly dirty white. Undertail coverts buff. Chin and throat whitish with dark brown streak down side of throat separating the throat from a white malar streak. White eye-ring. Entire lower mandible yellowish. Legs flesh coloured. Upper tail coverts have reddish-brown tinge.

6. Tickell's Blue Flycatcher *Cyornis tickelliae*
   රන්ළය නිල්-මැසිමාරා
   14cm. **Male:** Blue-black above. Bluish forehead, supercilium and shoulders. Throat, breast orange-brown. Belly white. **Female:** Duller, breast often paler less colourful.

7. Jerdon's Leafbird *Chloropsis jerdoni*
   ජරදන් කොළරිසියා
   18cm. **Male:** Yellowish forehead and sides of neck; black throat. **Female:** Throat bluish green.

8. Golden-fronted Leafbird *Chloropsis aurifrons*
   රන් නලල් කොළරිසියා
   19cm. Plumage completely green. Golden forehead. Bluish throat with black border, extending beyond the eye.

Plate 105

1. **Thick-billed Flowerpecker** *Dicaeum agile*
   මාතුඩු පිළිලිච්චා
   9cm. Short stubby bill. Brown streaks on sides of throat. White-tipped tail; reddish brown eye, white chin and throat.

2. **Pale-billed Flowerpecker** *Dicaeum erythrorhynchos*
   ළාතුඩු පිළිලිච්චා
   8cm. Thin pointed slightly down-curved bill and very pale grey underparts. Smallest bird in Sri Lanka.

3. **Purple-rumped Sunbird** *Nectarinia zeylonica*
   නිතඹ දම් සූටික්කා
   10cm. Slightly decurved short bill. **Male:** Purple rump, glossy green crown and shoulder patch. **Female and Juv:** Olive brown upperparts and dull yellow underparts.

4. **Purple Sunbird** *Nectarinia asiatica*
   දම් සූටික්කා
   10cm. Shorter bill than in "Long-billed Sunbird". **Male:** Blue-black belly. **Female:** Olive brown upperparts and dull yellow underparts.

5. **Long-billed Sunbird** *Nectarinia lotenia*
   දික්තුඩු සූටික්කා
   13cm. Long down-curved bill. **Male:** Glossy black upperparts with green sheen. Brown belly. **Female:** Olive brown upperparts and dull yellow underparts.

6. **House Sparrow** *Passer domesticus*
   ගේකුරුල්ලා
   15cm. **Male:** Grey crown, black throat, grey bill and chestnut nape. **Female:** Dull brown crown and pale eye brow.

7. **Baya Weaver** *Ploceus philippinus*
   රැක් වඩුකුරුල්ලා
   15cm. Unstreaked breast. The nest is pendulous and usually built over hanging ditches and water bodies.

8. **Streaked Weaver** *Ploceus manyar*
   පන් වඩුකුරුල්ලා
   15cm. Breast streaked with dark brown. **Male:** Yellow crown, dark brown face. **Female and Juv:** Pale eye brow.

Plate 106

1. **White-throated Munia** *Lonchura malabarica*
   ගෙලසුදු වීකුරුල්ලා
   10cm. Brown above. White rump. Tail blackish and pointed, long dark wings. Underparts creamy white with sides of belly brownish-buff. Bill thick and ashy black.

2. **White-rumped Munia** *Lonchura striata*
   නිතඹ සුදු වීකුරුල්ලා
   10cm. Black head, back tail and breast. White rump, lower breast and belly. Tail pointed. Bill bluish. Generally found in pairs and small flocks.

3. **Tricoloured Munia** *Lonchura malacca*
   තෙපැහැ වීකුරුල්ලා
   10cm. Black head and throat. Reddish-brown upperparts. Lower belly, undertail coverts black. Breast, upper belly white. Bill bluish-black.

4. **Scaly-breasted Munia** *Lonchura punctulata*
   ළය කායුරු වීකුරුල්ලා
   10cm. Reddish-brown face/throat. Brown/white scaled breast, belly and flanks. **Juv:** All brown with buff head.

5. **Forest Wagtail** *Dendronanthus indicus*
   වන-හැලපෙන්දා
   16cm. Dark brown above. Pale supercilium. Creamy yellow underparts. Dark brown bands on wing, throat and across breast. Bold upper breast band and crescentic lower breast bands on each side, almost meeting in middle.

6. **Yellow Wagtail** *Motacilla flava*
   කහ හැලපෙන්දා
   16cm. Upperparts greenish. Underparts bright yellow. Wings brownish with two whitish bars. Tail dark brown with white outer feathers. Five sub-species with variable head and upper back colour variations.

7. **Grey Wagtail** *Motacilla cinerea*
   අළු හැලපෙන්දා
   18cm. Head and back grey. White supercilium. Uppertail coverts greenish yellow. Narrow white wing bar. Outer tail feathers white. Inner tail feathers blackish brown. Underparts yellowish, brighter around vent.

8. **Paddyfield Pipit** *Anthus rufulus*
   කෙත් වැරටිච්චා
   17cm. Very much like Richard's Pipit, but shorter legs and slightly smaller.

Mammals

(Plates 107-115)

Amongst animals the group considered most "developed" are the Mammals. There are many aspects of their structure and activities that set mammals apart from other organisms Mammals form a distinct group of animals identified today by the possession of hair and, in females, mammary glands.

Mammals inhabit both terrestrial and marine habitats but land is their principal domain. Nevertheless, the largest animal in the world - the Blue Whale - is a marine mammal that breathes air.

The mammalian form and physiology have enabled these animals to live in very difficult conditions. The ability to control body temperature enables them to exist in very cold or very hot climates. Coupled with the ability to feed throughout the day they have been able to expand and increase in numbers, enabling mammals to establish themselves in nearly all the world's habitats.

For a small island of 65,000 sq.km. Sri Lanka has an impressive mammalian fauna, better than that of any island of similar size in the world. There are at least 125 known species of which 20 are endemic. It is the number of endemic species in Sri Lanka that are a special feature of the island's fauna.

The endemic mammals have an interesting distribution. Eight are confined entirely to the Wet Zone with the one endemic genus also confined to this zone. One mouse is confined to the Dry Zone, while the four primates are found widely distributed with subspecies in each zone.

PLATE 107

1. **Black-bearded Sheath-tailed Bat** *Taphozous melanopogon*
   රැවුල්කළු කැපුලුම්-වවුලා
   75-80mm. Forearm 61-64mm. In older males, black patches on the throat. The use tree holes, chimneys as their day roosts and usually they crawl on the surface, not hang like other bat species

2. **Bicoloured Leaf-nosed Bat** *Hipposideros ater*
   දෙපැහැ පත්නැහැ-වවුලා
   45-47mm. Forearm 36-37mm. Females slightly larger. Two thirds of the hair is white, while the tip is only coloured. When the fur is ruffled the white appears. Thus the "bicoloured' nature. It can easily recognized its smaller ear size shape and without supplementary leaflets. One pair to 20-50 individuals live together in their day roost.

3. **Schneider's Leaf-nosed Bat** *Hipposideros speoris*
   කෙස්කෙටි පත්නැහැ-වවුලා
   55-60mm. Forearm 50-54mm. Colour varies from greyish to bright golden brown. It can be recognized from its close relatives by the three supplementary leaflets and its smaller size. Sometimes several hundred have been found in the same colony. One of the most common bat species in the island, it can be found in abandoned houses and caves.

4. **Short-nosed Fruit Bat** *Cynopterus sphinx*
   තල-වවුලා
   10-13cm. Forearm 70-80mm. Easily identified from its closest relative by the narrow white margin on ear. This frugivorous species roost under "Thala palm" leaves during the day time.

Plate 108

1. **Indian Flying Fox** *Pteropus giganteus*
   මා වවුලා
   198-300mm, Forearm 152-183mm. The males have a reddish patch on the side of the neck and are larger. Upper side darker than underside. This frugivorous bat is the largest bat species in the island and can be seen hanging on the trees such as *Ficus, Cassia* etc.

2. **Fulvous Fruit Bat** *Rousettus leschenaulti*
   බෙරකහ පළ-වවුලා
   111-147mm. Forearm 75-86mm. Females smaller than males. Wing membrane blackish brown. The only cave-living fruit bat in Sri Lanka, it has some echolocating capabiities.

3. **Rufous Horse-shoe Bat** *Rhinolophus rouxii*
   බොරත් අස්ලාඩම්-වවුලා
   53-60mm. Forearm 47-54mm. Females smaller than males. General colour light brown. Upperside and closer to head darker. Wing membrane blackish brown. Uses abandoned houses and caves as a day roost.

4. **Pygmy Pipistrelle** *Pipistrellus tenuis*
   හීන් කොස්ඇට-වවුලා
   36-44mm. Forearm 26-30mm. Smallest bat species in the island. During daytime they hide within small crevices under roofs, down pipes, or tree holes as family groups (2-5). Wing membrane and body coffee brown to black.

5. **Painted Bat** *Kerivoula picta*
   විසිතුරු කිරි-වවුලා
   38-45mm. Forearm 31-33mm. Males slightly larger than females. Dorsal side bright orange. Underside paler. Wing membrane black with orange to reddish along the forearm. This is a very striking animal. Due to its colour pattern it can be easily recognize even in flight.

Plate 109

1. **Sri Lanka Purple-faced Leaf Monkey** *Semnopithecus vetulus* 🟢
   ශ්‍රී ලංකා කළු වඳුරා
   54-56cm. Tail 73cm. Generally sooty black with white whiskers. Nearly always found on trees, in the Dry Zone it likes to feed on trees near the rivers. Separated from the langurs by the round head and white whiskers. Four distinct subspecies recognized according to their body size, colour patterns, and geographical range. Endemic.

2. **Sri Lanka Toque Macaque** *Macaca sinica* 🟢
   ශ්‍රී ලංකා රිලවා
   47-49cm. Tail 59cm. General colour brown mixed with yellow. Troops consist of 10 to 20 individuals. Three distinct subspecies are recognized according to their body size, colour patterns, and geographical range.

3. **Grey Langur** *Semnopithecus priam*
   ඇලි වඳුරා
   62-64cm. Tail 68cm. General colour greyish. Tail held up (curved or 'S' shaped) when moving on the ground. The distinguishing feature is the pointed head, formed by the radiating hairs.

4. **Sri Lanka Red Slender Loris** *Loris tardigradus* 🟢
   ශ්‍රී ලංකා රත් උණහපුළුවා
   20cm. Females larger than males. Tail less. Yellowish brown. Eyes glow red when a flashlight is shone at them. Only use red light in the presence of these animals.

5. **Pangolin** *Manis crassicaudata*
   කබැල්ලෑවා
   89-141cm. Distinctive. Body colour varies with that of the local soil. Entirely nocturnal. It mainly feeds on termites and ants.

6. **Golden Jackal** *Canis aureus*
   හිවලා
   100cm. Brown tinged with reddish brown. Dark near mid-dorsal line of body, paler below, tail bushy, darker and held down. Usually found in pairs.

Plate 110

1. Jungle Cat *Felis chaus*
   වල් බළලා
   68cm. General colour sandy brown with a grey tinge. Darker above and lighter below. Ears tipped with black long hairs. Tail has black rings towards the tip. Dark stripes on legs which fade with age. Usually encountered when the cat crosses a road at night.

2. Leopard *Panthera pardus*
   කොටියා
   2.1m. Yellow with black rosettes. Sri Lankan subspecies is endemic.

3. Brown Mongoose *Herpestes fuscus*
   බොර මුගටියා
   65cm. Male larger. General colour brown; intensity varies according to the sub species from zone to zone. Tail carried with tip held up. Tail tip same colour as rest of body.

4. Striped-neck Mongoose *Herpestes vitticollis*
   මහ මුගටියා
   80cm. Male larger. Reddish brown. Tail often carried straight though it may be turned up at times. Tip of tail black. Black stripe behind ear.

5. Ruddy Mongoose *Herpestes smithii*
   රත් මුගටියා / හෝතම්බුවා
   65cm. Male larger. Tail carried with blackish tail tip held up. Active during day time.

Plate 111

1. **Otter** *Lutra lutra*
   දිය-බල්ලා
   90cm. Dark black-brown above. White underneath. Flat head. whiskers prominent. Occasionally seen in the pools of rivers during the early morning and late afternoon, but rarely seen at other times.

2. **Common Palm Civet** *Paradoxurus hermaphoditus*
   කලවැද්දා / උගුඩුවා
   1m. Colour highly variable. Generally blackish to grey. Often pale spots in a longitudinal row on the dorsal surface. Tail pure black. One of the common civets in the island which loves to eat toddy palm seed. It is also common in urban areas and during the day they shelter in shady trees or ceilings.

3. **Ring-tailed Civet** *Viverricula indica*
   උරුලෑවා
   89cm. Greyish brown with darker (brown) spots. Dorsal spots elongated forming longitudinal stripes. Black and white rings on the tail distinctive. Nocturnal species.

4. **Asian Elephant** *Elephas maximus*
   ඇතා / අලියා
   2.2-3.2m. Distinctive. Some males may have tusks. Females' hind body shape square, while in males it is tapering.

5. **Wild Buffalo** *Bubalus arnee*
   කුලු හරකා
   1.25m at shoulder. Males larger. Highly doubtful that pure wild buffaloes exist in Sri Lanka. Males with even partially wild blood have sweeping, broad horns.

Plate 112

1. **Spotted Deer** *Axis axis*
   තිත් මුවා
   1.2m at shoulder. Reddish brown to yellow brown with white spots on body. Underside white. Males develop a black neck band ventrally mainly during the rutting season. Branched antlers in males. Can be seen in large herds in open grassland and scrub.

2. **Porcupine** *Hystrix indica*
   ඉත්තෑවා
   79-89cm. Black and white quills on body and tail. Coarse, bristle like hair is present on the head and foreparts of the body. Nocturnal species, hides in rock crevices during the day time.

3. **Wild Boar** *Sus scrofa*
   වල් ඌරා
   95cm at shoulder. Males larger. Blackish. Young animals brown with black stripes on upper surface. Hair on the body is very scanty and bristle like. A mane is present, especially in the males. Usually found in herds with large numbers of piglets.

4. **Sri Lanka Mouse Deer** *Moschiola meminna* 🟢
   ශ්‍රී ලංකා මීමින්නා
   40cm at shoulder. In males the upper canines are elongated. Females larger. Brown with a greenish yellow (sandy) tinge, white underside. White spots on body, elongated and fused to form longitudinal bands on sides. Three white stripes on throat.

5. **Sambhur** *Cervus unicolor*
   ගෝනා
   1.3m. At shoulder. Males larger. Uniform dark brown with lighter underparts. Males have heavy antlers. Hair very coarse and shaggy. A mane is present in the males. Largest member of the deer family in Sri Lanka. It prefers jungles to open grasslands.

Plate 113

1. **Common Musk Shrew** *Suncus murinus*
   පොදු හික්-මීයා
   15-26cm. Bluish-grey to black mixed with reddish-brown above, paler bluish-grey to black below. Ears, muzzle, feet, and tail pinkish. Snout swollen on sides. Active at dusk. Insectivorous and, nightly, it can on more than its weight in insects.

2. **Soft-furred Metad** *Millardia meltada*
   කෙස්මුදු කෙත්-මීයා
   30cm. Rat with soft fur cover and shorter tail compare with head and body. Greyish brown to coffee brown color. Muzzle shorter than other rat species in the island. Especially likes wet areas, like tank catchments, near marshes, wet grasslands, and villus.

3. **White-tailed Rat** *Madromys blanfordi*
   වලිගසුදු වන-මීයා
   35cm. Two thirds distal part of the tail whitish. General appearance much more like House Mouse. Prefers rocky areas to thick jungles.

4. **Indian Field Mouse** *Mus booduga*
   වෙල් හීන්-මීයා
   16cm. Upper part dark brown and underparts whitish. Fur soft. Occurs in grassland, near wetlands, and in scrub.

5. **Sri Lanka Spiny Mouse** *Mus fernandoni* 🟢
   ශ්‍රී ලංකා කටු හීන්-මීයා
   18cm. Male slightly larger. Tail naked, dusky brown above, greyish below. Upperparts brownish red with a grey tinge, underparts grey to white, sometimes reddish brown wash on chest. Comparatively larger eyes and spiny hairs identify this rat.

Plate 114

1. **Indian House Mouse** *Mus musculus*
   ගේ හීන්-මීයා
   18cm. Much more like *M. booduga* but it differs in having an uniform greyish colour. Found in similar habitats as *M. booduga* and also common within houses.

2. **Black Rat** *Rattus rattus*
   පොදු ගේ මීයා
   48cm. General colour brownish red to blackish above, under surface variable. Common rat species in forests and also in the human settlements.

3. **Asiatic Long-tailed Climbing Mouse** *Vendeleuria oleracea*
   ගස්-මීයා
   21cm. Has a long prehensile tail. At night it can be seen in pairs or or individuals feeding on tall grass seeds (Illuk, Mana). It builds small nests among dense leaf branches or tree holes.

4. **Indian Gerbil** *Tatera indica*
   වැලි-මීයා
   42cm. Tail longer than head and body. Eyes large. Long hindfeet with well developed claws. Upper surface sandy brown, underparts white. Nocturnal. Usually can be seen on roadsides during the night.

Plate 115

1. **Palm Squirrel** *Funambulus palmarum*
   ලේනා
   31cm. Colour grizzled grey to black above, dirty white to yellow below. Three prominent cream coloured stripes on back.

2. **Sri Lanka Giant Squirrel** *Rattufa macroura*
   ශ්‍රී ලංකා දඩු ලේනා
   34-38cm Tail 36cm. Dry Zone subspecies: Grey brown above, dirty white below. Tail grey brown with white speckles reddish brown towards end. Wet Zone sub species-Blackish brown to jet black above, light orange yellow below, feet black, face pinkish. Tail black.

3. **Black-naped Hare** *Lepus nigricollis*
   වල් හාවා
   45-48cm. Females slightly larger, grey brown to brown. Black patch just behind ears. During the day time it hides within dense grass tussocks or under bushes. At night they come out and feed in the open grasslands and roadsides.

References

Ashton, M, Gunatilleke, S., de Zoysa, N., Dassanayake, M. D., Gunatilleke, N. & Wijesundara, S. (1997). *A field guide to the common trees and shrubs of Sri Lanka*. WHT Publications (Pvt) Limited for the Wildlife Heritage Trust of Sri Lanka, 95, Cotta Road, Colombo, Sri Lanka.

Bedjanic, M., Conniff, K., de Silva Wijeratne, G. 2007 Gehan's Photo Guide: *A Photographic Guide to the Dragonflies of Sri Lanka*. Jetwing Eco Holidays, Colombo.

Benjamin, S.P. and Bambaradeniya, C.N.B., 2006. Systematic and Conservation of Spider s in Sri Lanka: Current Status and Future Prospects; Fauna of Sri Lanka; Status of taxonomy, Research and Conservation. pp 53-58. Colombo: The World Conservation Union in Sri Lanka.

BirdLife International (2012) The BirdLife checklist of the birds of the world, with conservation status and taxonomic sources. Version 5.

Clayton, W. D., Dassanayake, M. D. & Fosberg, F. R. (1994). *A revised handbook to the flora of Ceylon (Vol. VIII)*. Amerind Publishing Co. Pvt. Ltd., 66 Janpath, New Delhi 110001.

Clayton, W. D., Dassanayake, M. D. & Fosberg, F. R. (1995). *A revised handbook to the flora of Ceylon (Vol. IX)*. Amerind Publishing Co. Pvt. Ltd., 66 Janpath, New Delhi 110001.

D' Abrera, B., 1998. *The Butterflies of Ceylon*. Melbourne London: Hill House Publishes.

Das, Indraneil & de Silva, Anslem 2005 *A photographic guide to snakes and other reptiles of Sri Lanka*. New Holland Publishers (UK) Ltd.

Dassanayake, M. D. & Clayton, W. D. (1996). *A revised handbook to the flora of Ceylon (Vol. X)*. Oxford & IBH Publishing Co. Ltd., 66 Janapath, New Delhi 110001.

Dassanayake, M. D. & Clayton, W. D. (1997). *A revised handbook to the flora of Ceylon (Vol. XI)*. Oxford & IBH Publishing Co. Ltd., New Delhi, Culcutta.

Dassanayake, M. D. & Clayton, W. D. (1998). *A revised handbook to the flora of Ceylon (Vol. XII)*. Oxford & IBH Publishing Co. Ltd., New Delhi, Culcutta.

Dassanayake, M. D. & Clayton, W. D. (1999). *A revised handbook to the flora of Ceylon (Vol. XIII)*. Oxford & IBH Publishing Co. Ltd., New Delhi, Culcutta.

Dassanayake, M. D. & Clayton, W. D. (2000). *A revised handbook to the flora of Ceylon (Vol. XIV)*. Oxford & IBH Publishing Co. Ltd., New Delhi, Culcutta.

Dassanayake, M. D. & Fosberg, F. R. (1980). *A revised handbook to the flora of Ceylon (Vol. I)*. Amerind Publishing Co. Pvt. Ltd., 66 Janpath, New Delhi 110001.

Dassanayake, M. D. & Fosberg, F. R. (1981). *A revised handbook to the flora of Ceylon (Vol. II)*. Amerind Publishing Co. Pvt. Ltd., 66 Janpath, New Delhi 110001.

Dassanayake, M. D. & Fosberg, F. R. (1981). *A revised handbook to the flora of Ceylon (Vol. III)*. Amerind Publishing Co. Pvt. Ltd., 66 Janpath, New Delhi 110001.

Dassanayake, M. D. & Fosberg, F. R. (1983). *A revised handbook to the flora of Ceylon (Vol. IV)*. Amerind Publishing Co. Pvt. Ltd., 66 Janpath, New Delhi 110001.

Dassanayake, M. D. & Fosberg, F. R. (1985). *A revised handbook to the flora of Ceylon (Vol. V).* Amerind Publishing Co. Pvt. Ltd., 66 Janpath, New Delhi 110001.

Dassanayake, M. D. & Fosberg, F. R. (1987). *A revised handbook to the flora of Ceylon (Vol. VI).* Amerind Publishing Co. Pvt. Ltd., 66 Janpath, New Delhi 110001.

Dassanayake, M. D. & Fosberg, F. R. (1991). *A revised handbook to the flora of Ceylon (Vol. VII).* Amerind Publishing Co. Pvt. Ltd., 66 Janpath, New Delhi 110001.

De Alwis Gunatilake, Samath 2007 [Freshwater Fishers of Sri Lanka] Biodiversity Secretariet, Ministry of Environment and Natural Resources, "Sampathpaya", 82, Rajamalwatta Road, Battaramulla.

De Fonseka, Terence 2000 *The dragonflies of Sri Lanka.* WHT Publication (Privet) Limited. 95, Cotta Road, Colombo 08.

De Silva Wijeratne, Gehan 2008 *A photographic guide to mammals of Sri Lanka.* New Holland Publishers (UK) Ltd.

De Silva, Anslem 2009 Amphibians of Sri Lanka: A photographic guide to common frogs, toads and Caecilians.

Downloaded, http://www.birdlife.info/im/species/checklist.

DWC (2008d). Biodiversity Baseline Survey: Uda Walawe National Park. Consultancy Services Report prepared by Green, M.J.B. (ed.), De Alwis, S.M.D.A.U., Dayawansa, P.N., How, R., U.K.G.K. Padmalal, Singhakumara, B.M.P., Weerakoon, D. and Wijesinghe, M.R. Infotechs IDEAS in association with GREENTECH Consultants. Sri Lanka Protected Areas Management and Wildlife Conservation Project (PAM&WCP/CONSULT/02/BDBS), Department of Wildlife Conservation, Ministry of Environment and Natural Resources, Colombo. 50 pp.

Foelix, R.F., 2011. Biology of Spiders 3rd Edition. Oxford university press.

Grimmett, R.,Inskipp, C. & Inskipp, T. 1998 *Birds of the Indian Subcontinent.* Christopher Helm, London.

Henry, G.M. 1998. *A guide to the birds of Sri Lanka.* 3rd ed. Oxford Univ. Press, New Delhi.

Inskipp, T., Lindsey, N. and Duckworth, W. 1996. *An annotated checklist of the birds of the oriental region.* Oriental Bird Club, Sandy.

Jocqué, R. and Dippenaar-Schoeman, A.S., 2006. Spider families of the World. Tervuren (Belgium): Peeters nv.

Kazmierczak, K. 2000 *A field guide to the birds of India,* Pica Press, Mountfield.

Kotagama, S.W. & Gamini Ratnavira. 2010 *An illustrated guide to the birds of Sri Lanka.* Field Ornithology Group of Sri Lanka, Colombo.

Kotagama, S.W. & Wijayasinha, A. S. 1998. සිරි ලක කුරුල්ලෝ [=Siri Laka Kurullo]. Wildlife Heritage Trust, Colombo.

Kotagama, S.W. & Wijayasinha, A. S. 2011. ශ්‍රී ලංකා කුරුල්ලෝ [=Siri Lanka Kurullo]. Field Ornithology Group of Sri Lanka, Colombo.

Kotagama, S.W. (Tamil Publication) 2012. இலங்கையின் பொதுப்பறவைகள் பறவைகளை அடையாளம் காண்பதற்கான கைநூல (=Common birds of Sri Lanka) Field Ornithology Group of Sri Lanka, Colombo.

Kotagama, Sarath 2004 *Mammals in Sri Lanka*. Field Ornithology Group of Sri Lanka, Deprtment of Zoology, University of Colombo, Colombo.

Kudavidanage, E.P. 2012 PhD Thesis, National university of Singapore.

Manamendra-Arachchi, Kelum & Pethiyagoda, Rohan 2006 [=Sri Lankawe Ubhayajiween] WHT Publication (Pvt) Ltd, Colombo.

Mendis, A.S. & Fernando, C.H. 1962 *A guide to the freshwater fauna of Ceylon with a forwarded, additional updatng on fishes, amphibia and selected references* by Fernando, C.H & Weerawardhena, S.R. ed., 2002. Fisheries research station, Ceylon.

Mendis, A.S. & Fernando, C.H. 1962 *A guide to the freshwater fauna of Ceylon with a forwarded, additional updatng on fishes, amphibia and selected references* by Fernando, C.H & Weerawardhena, S.R. ed., 2002. Fisheries research station, Ceylon.Ormiston, W., 1924. The Butterflies of Ceylon. Colombo: H.W. Cave & Co.

Pathirana, H.D.N.C., 1980, Geology of Sri Lanka in relation to Plate Tectonics; L. Natn. Sci. Coun. Sri Lanka v. 8, p. 75-85

Perera, D.G.A. & Kotagama, S.W. 1983. *A systematic nomenclature for the birds of Sri Lanka*. Field Ornithology Group of Sri Lanka, Colombo.

Perera, W.P.N. and Bambaradeniya, C.N.B., 2006. Species richness, Distribution and Conservation Status of Butterflies in Sri Lanka; Fauna of Sri Lanka; Status of taxonomy, Research and Conservation. pp 53-58. Colombo: The World Conservation Union in Sri Lanka.

Pethiyagoda, R. 1991. Fresh Water Fishes of Sri Lanka. Wildlife Heritage Trust, Colombo. 362pp.

Philips, W.W.A. 1935. *Manual of the mammals of Ceylon*. Dulau & Co., London.

Pocock, R.I., 1900. *The Fauna of British India, Including Ceylon and Burma*, Arachnida. London: Taylor and Francis.

Samarasinghe, M.D.P. Paranagama, P. & Veediyabandara, S., 1998. Survey of the butterfly fauna of Udawalawe National Park. Proceedings of the 2nd Annual Forestry Symposium 1996; Department of Forestry and Environmental Science, University of Sri Jayawardanapura, Sri Lanka.

Samarawckrama, V. A. M. P. K. Janananda, M. D. B. G. Ranawana, K. B. & Smith, A, 2005. Study of the distribution of the genus Poecilotheria of the Family Theraphosidae in Sri Lanka. Cey. J. Sci. (Bio. Sci.) Vol 34, 2005, 75-86.

Senaratna, L. K. (2001). A checklist of the flowering plants of Sri Lanka. National Science Foundation of Sri Lanka, 47/5, Maitland Place, Colombo 07, Sri Lanka.

Sibley, C. G. & Monroe, B.L. 1990. *Distribution and taxonomy of the birds of the world*. Yale Univ. Press, New Haven & London.

Simpson, M. G. (2006). Plant Systematics. Elsevier Academic Press, 30 Corporate Drive, Suite 400, Burlington, MA 01803, USA.

Somaweera, Ruchira & Somaweera, Nilusha 2009 *Lizards of Sri Lanka - A Colour Guide with Field Keys*. Andreas S. Brahm, Heddernheimer Landstr. 20, 60439 Frankfurt am Main, Germany.

Talbot, G., 1939. *The Fauna of British India, Including Ceylon and Burma Butterflies Vol. 1 & 2*. Third Indian reprint edition, 1986. New Delhi: Today & Tomorrow's Printers and Publishers.

Toman, J & Felix, J 1974. *A Field Guide in Colour to Palnts and Animals*. Octopus Books Limited.

Van Nieukerken, E. K. et al, 2011. Order Lepidoptera Linnaeus, 1758. In: Zhang, Z.-Q. (Ed.) Animal biodiversity: An outline of higher-level classification and survey of taxonomic richness. Zootaxa 3148: 212-221.

Vlas, J. & J. de. (2008). *Illustrated field guide to the flowers of Sri Lanka*. Mark Booksellers and Distributors (Pvt) Ltd, Kandy.

Warakagoda D, Carol Inskipp, Tim Inskipp, Richard Grimmett. 2012. *Birds of Sri Lanka. Helm Field Guide*. Christopher Helm, London.

Woodhouse, L.G.O., 1950. *The Butterfly fauna of Ceylon 2nd Edition*. Colombo: The Ceylon Government Press.

Index

Index of Plants

Numbers refer to plate numbers and illustration numbers, not page numbers.

Scientific Names

Acacia leucophloea **32: 2**
Alseodaphne semecarpifolia **14: 1**
Argyreia osyrensis **6: 1**
Atalantia monophylla **24: 1**
Azadirachta indica **16: 3**
Barleria prionitis **1: 1**
Bauhinia racemosa **10: 2**
Bauhinia tomentosa **10: 3**
Benkara malabarica **21: 2**
Bridelia retusa **8: 2**
Calotropis gigantea **3: 2**
Canthium coromandelicum **21: 3**
Capparis zeylanica **32: 3**
Carissa spinarum **2: 3**
Carmona retusa **4: 1**
Cassia auriculata **11: 1**
Cassia roxburghii **11: 2**
Catunaregam spinosa **22: 1**
Chloroxylon swietenia **24: 2**
Cissus quadrangularis **30: 3**
Cissus vitiginea **31: 1**
Clausena indica **31: 3**
Connarus monocarpus **5: 3**
Crateva adansonii **4: 3**
Crinum defixum **1: 3**
Crotalaria spp. **11: 3**
Dendrophthoe falcata **15: 2**
Derris parviflora **12: 1**
Derris scandens **12: 2**
Dichrostachys cinerea **12: 3**
Dillenia indica **6: 2**
Dimorphocalyx glabellus **8: 3**
Diospyros ebenum **7: 1**
Diospyros montana **7: 2**
Diospyros ovalifolia **7: 3**
Drypetes sepiaria **9: 1**
Ehretia laevis **4: 2**
Erythroxylum zeylanicum **33: 1**

Eucalyptus spp. **18: 2**
Eugenia bracteata **18: 3**
Eupatorium odoratum **34: 3**
Euphorbia antiquorum **9: 2**
Ficus benghalensis **17: 2**
Flueggea leucopyrus **9: 3**
Gloriosa superba **5: 1**
Glycosmis mauritiana **24: 3**
Gmelina asiatica **28: 3**
Grewia damine **27: 3**
Grewia orientalis **28: 1**
Haldina cordifolia **22: 2**
Hibiscus micranthus **15: 3**
Holoptelea integrifolia **28: 2**
Hopea cordifolia **6: 3**
Hugonia mystax **14: 2**
Jasminum auriculatum **19:3**
Lantana camara **29: 1**
Lepisanthes tetraphylla **26: 2**
Limonia acidissima **25: 1**
Maba buxifolia **8: 1**
Mallotus rhamnifolius **33: 3**
Mangifera zeylanica **2: 1**
Manilkara hexandra **27: 2**
Memecylon angustifolium **16: 1**
Memecylon umbellatum **16: 2**
Miliusa indica **34: 1**
Mitragyna parviflolia **22: 3**
Morinda coreia **23: 1**
Murraya paniculata **25: 2**
Mussaenda frondosa **23: 2**
Ochna lanceolata **19: 2**
Panicum maximum **20: 1**
Paramignya monophylla **25: 3**
Phoenix pusilla **3: 1**
Phyllanthus polyphyllus **10: 1**
Pleiospermium alatum **26: 1**
Polyalthia korinti **2: 2**

Pongamia pinnata **13: 1**
Premna tomentosa **29: 2**
Pterospermum suberifolium **31: 2**
Salacia reticulata **34: 2**
Sapindus emarginata **26: 3**
Schleichera oleosa **27: 1**
Scutia myrtina **20: 2**
Stenosiphonium cordifolium **1: 2**
Stereospermum colais **32: 1**
Streblus asper **17: 3**
Streblus taxoides **18: 1**
Strychnos nux-vomica **14: 3**
Strychnos potatorum **15: 1**
Syzygium cumini **19: 1**
Tamarindus indica **13: 2**
Tarenna asiatica **23: 3**
Tectona grandis **29: 3**
Terminalia arjuna **5: 2**
Toddalia asiatica **33: 2**
Uraria picta **13: 3**
Ventilugo madraspatana **20: 3**
Vitex altissima **30: 1**
Vitex negundo **30: 2**
Walsura trifoliolata **17: 1**
Wattakaka volubilis **3: 3**
Ziziphus oenoplia **21: 1**

Index of Molluscs

Numbers refer to plate numbers and illustration numbers, not page numbers.

Scientific Names

Aulopoma itieri var. *hofmeisteri* 36: 7
Beddomea trifasciatus 36: 1
Bellamya ceylonica 35: 4
Bithynia inconspicus 35: 2
Cryptozona bistrialis 36: 6
Euplecta spp. 36: 2
Eurychlamys vilipensa 36: 5
Indoplanorbis exustus 35: 6
Lamellidens marginalis 35:8
Lymnaea pinguis 35: 7
Melanoides tuberculata 35: 5
Micraulax coeloconus 36: 10
Mirus panos 36: 4
Paludomus zeylanica 35: 1
Pila globosa 35: 3
Pterocyclus troscheli 36: 8
Rhachistia pulcher 36: 3
Theobaldius spp. 36: 9

Index of Arthropoda

Numbers refer to plate numbers and illustration numbers, not page numbers.

Scientific Names

Acheta spp. **39: 5**
Anisops barbata **37: 4**
Anophiline (Mosquito) Larvae **38: 2**
Apis cerena **41: 1**
Apis dorsata **41: 2**
Apis florae **41: 3**
Blatta spp. **39: 9**
Coccinella spp. **39: 7**
Cybister (Water Beetle) Larvae **38: 6**
Cybister spp. **37: 5**
Distoleon tetragrammicus **40: 3**
Dysdercus ungulates **39: 2**
Eumenes coarctatus **41: 7**
Forficula spp. **39: 8**
Gerris adelaidis **37: 8**
Gyrinus spp. **37: 3**
Gyroptalpa spp. **39: 10**
Heterometrus swarmmerdami **40: 6**
Hydrocoptus spp. **37: 6**
Julis spp. (Millipede) **40: 2-i, 2-ii, 2-iii**
Laccotrephes grossus **37: 7**
Lethocerus indicus **37: 1**
Luciola spp. **39: 3**
Luciola spp. **40: 4**
Macrobrachium rosenbergii **37: 10**
Mantis spp. **39: 4**
Neuroptera (Alderfly) Larvae **38: 3**
Odonata (Damselfly) Larvae **38: 4**
Odonata (Dragonfly) Larvae **38: 5**
Odonata (Mayfly) Larvae **38: 7**
Parathelpheus spps;
Ceylonothalpheus spp, etc **37: 11**
Ranatra filiformis **37: 9**
Rhipicephalus microplus **40: 5**
Scolopander spp. **40: 1**
Sphaeroderma rusticum **37: 2**
Tethigonia spp. **39: 1**
Tibicen spp. **39: 6**

Trichoptera (Caddisfly) Larvae **38: 1**
Trigona iridipennis **41: 4**
Vespa orientalis **41: 6**
Xylocopa tenuiscapa **41: 5**

Index of Dung beetles
Numbers refer to plate numbers and illustration numbers, not page numbers.

Scientific Names

Catharsius molossus **42: 3**
Copris signatus **42: 2**
Copris sodalis **42: 4**
Onthophagus difficilis **42: 6**
Onthophagus gazella **42: 5**
Onthophagus militaris **42: 7**
Onthophagus spinifex **42: 8**
Onthophagus unifasciatus **42: 9**
Paragymnopleurus koenegi **42: 1**
Paragymnopleurus melanarius **42: 10**

Index of Spiders

Numbers refer to plate numbers and illustration numbers, not page numbers.

Common Names

Ant-like Jumper, Giant **45: 6**
Red **45: 7**
Crab Spider, Sri Lanka Elongated Green **45: 1**
White Flower **45: 3**
Dewdrop Spider, Red and silver **44: 3**
Fishing Spider, Six-spotted **44: 6**
Fly Catcher, Common House **45: 2**
Funnel-weaver, Grass **44: 5**
Funnel-web Spider, Grass **44: 7**
Huntsman Spider, Domestic **44: 8**
Kite Spider, Common **43: 4**
Long-jawed Orbweaver, Common **43: 7**
Lynx Spider, Yellow-striped **44: 4**
Phintella, Banded **45: 4**
Sailor Spider, Brown **43: 3**
Spider, Hermit **44: 2**
Signature **43: 5**
Spiny-orb Weaver, Common **43: 4**
Telamonia, Two-striped **45: 8**
Tiger Spider, Sri Lanka Pedersen's **43: 1**
Tiny Jumper, Red & blue **45: 5**
Tree trunk Spider, Ornate **43: 2**
Two-tailed Spider, Common **44: 1**
Wood Spider, Giant **43: 6**

Scientific Names

Argiope anasuja **43: 5**
Argyrodes flavescens **44: 3**
Dolomedes (cf.) triton **44: 6**
Gasteracantha geminata **43: 4**
Herennia multipuncta **43: 2**
Hersilia sevignyi **44: 1**
Heteropoda venatoria **44: 8**
Hippasa greenalliae **44: 7**
Myrmarachne maxillosea **45: 6**
Myrmarachne palataleoides **45: 7**
Neoscona nautica **43: 3**
Nephila pilipes **43: 6**
Nephilengys malabarensis **44: 2**
Oxyopes macilentus **44: 4**
Oxytate subvirens **45: 1**
Phintella vittata **45: 4**
Plexippus petersi **45: 2**
Poecilotheria pederseni **43: 1**
Siler semiglaucus **45: 5**
Tegenaria domestica **44: 5**
Telamonia dimidiata **45: 8**
Tetragnatha viridorufa **43: 7**
Thomisus spectabilis **45: 3**

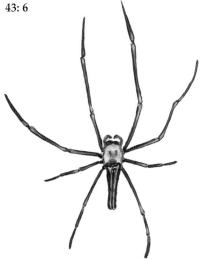

Index of Dragonflies & Damselflies

Numbers refer to plate numbers and illustration numbers, not page numbers.

Common Names	Scientific Names
Basker, Scarlet **48: 2**	*Acisoma panorpoides* **47: 4**
Bluetail, Common **49: 4**	*Agriocnemis pygmaea* **50: 2**
Dropwing, Crimson **46: 4**	*Brachythemis contaminata* **47: 5**
Dancing **46: 2**	*Bradinopyga geminata* **50: 5**
Featherleg, Yellow **50: 4**	*Ceriagrion coromandelianum* **49: 3**
Flangetail, Rapacious **48: 5**	*Copera marginipes* **50: 4**
Flutterer, Variegated **47: 2**	*Crocothemis servilia* **48: 1**
Gem, Green's **49: 2**	*Diplacodes nebulosa* **48: 4**
Ultima **50: 3**	*Diplacodes trivialis* **48: 3**
Glider, Sociable **47: 1**	*Ichtinogomphus rapax* **48: 5**
Wandering **46: 5**	*Ischnura senegalensis* **49: 4**
Groundling, Asian **47: 5**	*Libellago finalis* **50: 3**
Parasol, Pied **49: 1**	*Libellago greeni* **49: 2**
Percher, Black-tipped **48: 4**	*Neurothemis tullia* **49: 1**
Blue **48: 3**	*Orthetrum pruinosum* **46: 3**
Pintail, Asian **47: 4**	*Orthetrum sabina* **46: 1**
Pursuer, Blue **47: 3**	*Pantala flavescens* **46: 5**
Rockdweller, Indian **50: 5**	*Potamarcha congener* **47: 3**
Scarlet, Oriental **48: 1**	*Pseudagrion malabaricum* **49: 5**
Skimmer, Green **46: 1**	*Pseudagrion rubriceps* **50: 1**
Pink **46: 3**	*Rhyothemis variegata* **47: 2**
Sprite, Malabar **49: 5**	*Tramea limbata* **47: 1**
Sprite, Orange-faced **50: 1**	*Trithemis aurora* **46: 4**
Waxtail, Yellow **49: 3**	*Trithemis pallidinervis* **46: 2**
Wisp, Wandering **50: 2**	*Urothemis signata* **48: 2**

Index of Butterflies

Numbers refer to plate numbers and illustration numbers, not page numbers.

Common Names

Acaciablue, Common **56: 5**
Albatross, Common **52: 2**
Angle, Golden **60: 8**
Apefly **56: 2**
Awl, Brown **60: 2**
Awlet, Branded Orange **60: 1**
Baron **55: 2**
Birdwing, Sri Lanka **51: 1**
Blue, Gram **59: 6**
    Lime **59: 7**
    Pea **58: 5**
    Zebra **58: 6**
Bob, Chestnut **60: 11**
    Indian Palm **60: 10**
Bushbrown, Common **55: 9**
Butterfly, Lime **51: 5**
Castor, Angled **53: 7**
    Tawny **53: 6**
Cerulean, Common **58: 3**
    Dark **58: 1**
    Metallic **58: 2**
Ciliateblue, Pointed **57: 7**
Clipper **55: 1**
Commander **54: 10**
Cornelian **57: 6**
Crow, Common **53: 5**
Cruiser **53: 10**
Cupid, Indian **59: 2**
Dart, Tropic **61: 3**
Dartlet, Common **61: 2**
Demon, Common Banded **60: 12**
Eggfly, Danaid **54: 6**
Eveningbrown, Common **55: 6**
Flat, Ceylon Snow **60: 7**
    Common Small **60: 6**
    Sri Lanka Black **60: 4**
    Tricolour Pied **60: 5**
Flitter, Tree **60: 13**

Forget-me-not **58: 4**
Four-ring, White **55: 10**
Grassblue, Lesser **58: 9**
    Tiny **58: 10**
Grassdart, Common **61: 1**
Grass-yellow, Common **52: 10**
    Small **52: 9**
    Three-spot **53: 1**
Guavablue, Common **57: 5**
Gull, Common **52: 1**
Hedgeblue, Common **59: 3**
Hopper, Bush **60: 9**
Immigrant, Mottled **52: 5**
Imperial, Common **57: 1**
Jewel, Grass **58: 8**
Jezebel **51: 9**
Judy, Plum **59: 8**
Lady, Painted **54: 3**
Leafblue, Purple **56: 7**
Leopard **53: 9**
Lineblue, Common **57: 10**
    Dingy **57: 8**
    Sri Lanka Pale 6- **57: 9**
Malayan **59: 5**
Mine **51: 7**
Mormon, Blue **51: 6**
Nawab **55: 4**
Nigger **55: 8**
Nymph, Tree **53: 2**
Oakblue, Centaur **56: 4**
Oakleaf, Sri Lanka Blue **54: 7**
Orange-tip, Great **52: 4**
    Little **52: 8**
    White **52: 3**
Palmdart, Pale **61: 4**
Palmfly, Common **56: 1**
Pansy, Grey **54: 4**
    Peacock **54: 5**

Peacock, Banded 51: 4
Pierrot, Common 58: 7
    Red 59: 1
Pioneer 51: 10
Plane 57: 4
Prince, Black 55: 3
Psyche 51: 8
Puzzle, Monkey 56: 10
Quaker 59: 4
Rajah, Tawny 55: 5
Redeye, Common 60: 14
    Giant 60: 3
Redspot 56: 6
Rose, Common 51: 3
    Crimson 51: 2
Rustic 53: 8
Sailor, Chestnut-streaked 54: 9
    Common 54: 8
Salmon-arab, Small 52: 7
Silverline, Common 57: 2
Skipper, Indian 60: 15
Sunbeam, Indian 56: 3
Swift, Conjoined 61: 5
    Smallest 61: 6
Tiger, Glassy 53: 3
    Plain 53: 4
Tinsel, Common 56: 8
Tit, Nilgiri 57: 3
Treebrown, Common 55: 7
Wanderer, Dark 52: 6
Wing, Lace 54: 2
Yamfly 56: 9
Yeoman, Tamil 54: 1

Scientific Names

Abisara echerius 59: 8
Acraea violae 53: 6
Actyolepis puspa felderi 59: 3
Amblypodia anita 56: 7
Amittia dioscorides singa 60: 9
Anthene lycaenina 57: 7
Appias albina 52: 2
Arhopala pseudocentaurus 56: 4
Ariadne ariadne 53: 7
Badamia exclamationis 60: 2
Belenois aurota 51: 10
Bibasis oedipodea ataphus 60: 1
Bindahara phocides 57: 4
Caprona ransonnettii ransonnettii 60: 8
Castalius rosimon 58: 7
Catapaecilma major 56: 8
Catochrysops strabo 58: 4
Catopsilia pyranthe 52: 5
Celaenorrhinus spilothyrus 60: 4
Cepora nerissa 52: 1
Cethosia nietneri 54: 2
Charaxes psaphon 55: 5
Cheritra freja 57: 1
Chilades lajus 59: 7
Chilasa clytia 51: 7
Cirrochroa thais 54: 1
Coladenia indrani 60: 5
Colotis amata 52: 7
Colotis etrida 52: 8
Cupha erymanthis 53: 8
Curetis thetis 56: 3
Danaus chrysippus 53: 4
Delias eucharis 51: 9
Deudorix epijarbas 57: 6
Elymnias hypermnestra 56: 1
Euchrysops cnejus 59: 6
Euploea core 53: 5
Eurema blanda 53: 1
Eurema brigitta 52: 9
Eurema hecabe 52: 10

Euthalia aconthea 55: 2
Everes lacturnus 59: 2
Freyeria trochilus 58: 8
Gangara thyrsis clothilda 60: 3
Hebomoia glaucippe 52: 4
Hyarotis adrastus 60: 13
Hypolimnas misippus 54: 6
Hypolycaena nilgirica 57: 3
Iambrix salsala luteipalpus 60: 11
Idea iasonia 53: 2
Ixias marianne 52: 3
Jamides alecto 58: 2
Jamides bochus 58: 1
Jamides celeno 58: 3
Junonia almana 54: 5
Junonia atlites 54: 4
Kallima philarchus 54: 7
Lampides boeticus 58: 5
Leptosia nina 51: 8
Lethe rohria 55: 7
Loxura atymnus 56: 9
Matapa aria 60: 14
Megisba malaya 59: 5
Melannitis leda 55: 6
Moduza procris 54: 10
Mycalesis perseus 55: 9
Nacaduba sinhala 57: 9
Neopithicops zalmora 59: 4
Neptis hylas 54: 8
Neptis jumbah 54: 9
Notocrypta paralysos alysia 60: 12
Oriens goloides 61: 2
Orsotriaena medus 55: 8
Pachliopta aristolochiae 51: 3
Pachliopta hector 51: 2
Papilio crino 51: 4
Papilio demoleus 51: 5
Papilio polymnestor 51: 6
Parantica aglea 53: 3
Pareronia ceylanica 52: 6
Parnara bada bada 61: 6
Parthenos sylvia 55: 1

Pelopidas conjuncta narooa 61: 5
Petrelaea dana 57: 8
Phalanta phalantha 53: 9
Polyura athamas 55: 4
Potanthus confuscius satra 61: 3
Prosotas nora 57: 10
Rathinda amor 56: 10
Rohana parisatis 55: 3
Sarangesa dasahara aibicilia 60: 6
Spalgis epeus 56: 2
Spalia galba 60: 15
Spindasis vulcanus 57: 2
Suastus gremius subgrisea 60: 10
Surendra vivarna 56: 5
Syntarucus plinius 58: 6
Tagiades japetus obscurus 60: 7
Talicada nyseus 59: 1
Taractrocera maevius 61: 1
Telicota colon amba 61: 4
Troides darsius 51: 1
Vanessa cardui 54: 3
Vindula erota 53: 10
Virachola isocrates 57: 5
Ypthima ceylonica 55: 10
Zesius chrysomallus 56: 6
Zizina otis 58: 9
Zizula hylax 58: 10

Index of Fishes

Numbers refer to plate numbers and illustration numbers, not page numbers.

Common Names	Scientific Names
Barb, Long-snouted **67: 1**	*Amblypharyngodon melettinus* **65: 1**
Redside **66: 3**	*Catla catla* **67: 5**
Silver **66: 4**	*Chamma gachua* **63: 2**
Sri lanka Filamented **66: 2**	*Channa punctata* **63: 3**
Sri Lanka Flying **65: 3**	*Channa striata* **63: 4**
Sri lanka Olive **66: 1**	*Cirrhinus mrigala* **67: 4**
Sri Lanka Swamp **66: 5**	*Ctenopharyngodon idella* **67: 3**
Carp, Grass **67: 3**	*Dawkinsia sinhala* **66: 2**
Carplet, Silver **65: 1**	*Devario malabaricus* **65: 2**
Catfish, Butter **62: 3**	*Esomus thernoicos* **65: 3**
Stinging **62: 2**	*Etroplus maculatus* **64: 1**
Striped Dwarf **62: 4**	*Etroplus suratensis* **64: 2**
Catla **67: 5**	*Garra ceylonensis* **63: 1**
Chromide, Orange **64: 1**	*Glossogobius giuris* **62: 5**
Danio, Giant **65: 2**	*Heteropneustes fossilis* **62: 2**
Goby, Bar-eyed **62: 5**	*Labeo dussumieri* **65: 5**
Gourami, Giant **64: 3**	*Labeo rohita* **65: 6**
Halfbeak **62: 1**	*Mystus vittatus* **62: 4**
Labeo, Common **65: 5**	*Ompok bimaculatus* **62: 3**
Mahseer **67: 2**	*Oreochromis mossambicus* **64: 4**
Mrigal **67: 4**	*Oreochromis niloticus* **64: 5**
Murrel **63: 4**	*Osphronemus goramy* **64: 3**
Rasbora, Stripped **65: 4**	*Puntius bimaculatus* **66: 3**
Rohu **65: 6**	*Puntius dorsalis* **67: 1**
Snakehead, Brown **63: 2**	*Puntius thermalis* **66: 5**
Spotted **63: 3**	*Puntius vittatus* **66: 4**
Spot, Pearl **64: 2**	*Rasbora microchephala* **65: 4**
Sucker, Sri Lanka Stone **63: 1**	*Systomus timbiri* **66: 1**
Tilapia **64: 4**	*Tor khudree* **67: 2**
Tilapia **64: 5**	*Zenarchopterus dispar* **62: 1**

Index of Amphibians

Numbers refer to plate numbers and illustration numbers, not page numbers.

Common Names	Scientific Names
Frog, Common Bull **68: 2**	*Duttaphrynus melanostictus* **68: 1**
Common Paddyfield **69: 5**	*Euphlyctis cyanophlyctis* **68: 6**
Indian Skipper **68: 6**	*Euphlyctis hexadactylus* **69: 1**
Jerdon's Bull **69: 2**	*Fejervarya limnocharis* **69: 5**
Ornate Narrow-mouth **68: 3**	*Haylarana gracilis* **69: 6**
Red Narrow-mouth **68: 4**	*Hoplobatrachus crassus* **69: 2**
Six-toed Green **69: 1**	*Kaloula taprobanica* **68: 2**
White-bellied Pug-snout **68: 5**	*Microhyla ornata* **68: 3**
Toad, Common **68: 1**	*Microhyla rubra* **68: 4**
Tree frog, Common Hour-glass **69: 3**	*Polypedates cruciger* **69: 3**
Spotted **69: 4**	*Polypedates maculatus* **69: 4**
Wood frog, Sri Lanka **69: 6**	*Ramanella variegata* **68: 5**

Index of Reptiles

Numbers refer to plate numbers and illustration numbers, not page numbers.

Common Names

Cobra, Spectacled 71: 6
Crocodile, Mugger 75: 1
Gecko, Bark 73: 1
    Common House 73: 4
    Four-claw 73: 5
    Sri Lanka Kandyan 73: 2
    Sri Lanka Spotted House 73: 3
Keelback, Buff-striped 70: 3
    Checkered 71: 4
    Olive 70: 5
Lizard, Common Garden 72: 1
Lizard, Green Garden 72: 2
    Sri Lanka Lowland Kangaroo 72: 4
    Sri Lanka Painted-lip 72: 3
Monitor, Land 74: 5
    Water 74: 4
Python, Rock 70: 1
Skink, Bronzegreen Little 74: 2
    Common 74: 1
    Sri Lanka Common Supple 74: 3
Snake, Beddome's Cat 70: 4
    Common Bronzeback Tree 71: 2
    Common Rat 71: 3
    Forsten's Cat 70: 6
    Green Vine 70: 2
    Sri Lanka Flying 70: 7
    Trinket 71: 1
Tortoise, Star 75: 4
Turtle, Black 75: 2
    Sri Lanka Flapshell 75: 3
Viper, Hump-nosed Pit 71: 7
    Russell's 71: 5

Scientific Names

Ahaetulla nasuta 70: 2
Amphiesma stolatum 70: 3
Atretium schistosum 70: 5
Boiga beddomei 70: 4
Boiga forsteni 70: 6
Calotes calotes 72: 2
Calotes ceylonensis 72: 3
Calotes versicolor 72: 1
Chrysopelea taprobanica 70: 7
Coelognathus helena 71: 1
Crocodylus paluster 75: 1
Daboia russelii 71: 5
Dendrelaphis tristis 71: 2
Eutropis carinata lankae 74: 1
Eutropis macularia macularia 74: 2
Gehyra mutilata 73: 5
Geochelone elegans 75: 4
Hemidactylus depressus 73: 2
Hemidactylus frenatus 73: 4
Hemidactylus leschenaultii 73: 1
Hemidactylus parvimaculatus 73: 3
Hypnale hypnale 71: 7
Lankascincus fallax 74: 3
Lissemys ceylonensis 75: 3
Melanochelys trijuga 75: 2
Naja naja 71: 6
Otocryptis nigristigma 72: 4
Ptyas mucosa 71: 3
Python molurus 70: 1
Varanus bengalensis 74: 5
Varanus salvator 74: 4
Xenochrophis piscator 71: 4

Index of Birds

Numbers refer to plate numbers and illustration numbers, not page numbers.

Common Names

Adjutant, Lesser **78: 5**
Babbler, Dark-fronted **103: 4**
  Sri Lanka Brown-capped **103: 1**
  Tawny-bellied **103: 2**
  Yellow-billed **103: 6**
  Yellow-eyed **103: 5**
Barbet, Brown-headed **96: 3**
  Coppersmith **96: 4**
  Crimson-fronted **96: 5**
Bee-eater, Blue-tailed **94: 3**
  Chestnut-headed **94: 5**
  Little Green **94: 4**
Besra **82: 5**
Bittern, Black **79: 5**
  Cinnamon **79: 1**
  Yellow **79: 2**
Bulbul, Asian Black **102: 4**
  Black-crested **102: 1**
  Red-vented **102: 3**
  White-browed **102: 2**
Bushlark, Jerdon's **100: 4**
Buttonquail, Barred **76: 2**
Cisticola, Zitting **101: 1**
Coot, Common **84: 3**
Cormorant, Great **81: 4**
  Indian **81: 3**
  Little **81: 2**
Coucal, Greater **91: 5**
Crow, House **100: 2**
  Jungle **100: 1**
Cuckoo, Banded Bay **90: 4**
  Chestnut-winged **90: 1**
  Drongo **90: 6**
  Grey-bellied **90: 5**
  Indian **90: 3**
  Pied **90: 2**
Cuckooshrike, Large **98: 4**
  Black-headed **98: 5**

Darter, Oriental **81: 5**
Dove, Emerald **88: 3**
Dove, Spotted **88: 2**
Drongo, Greater Racket-tailed **99: 3**
Drongo, White-bellied **99: 2**
Eagle, Crested Serpent **83: 4**
Eagle-owl, Spot-bellied **92: 2**
Egret, Cattle **80: 3**
Egret, Great **80: 2**
Egret, Intermediate **80: 1**
Egret, Little **80: 4**
Fantail, White-browed **99: 6**
Fish-eagle, Grey-headed **83: 1**
Fish-owl, Brown **92: 3**
Flameback, Black-rumped **97: 5**
Flameback, Greater **97: 6**
Flowerpecker, Pale-billed **105: 2**
Flowerpecker, Thick-billed **105: 1**
Flycatcher, Asian Brown **104: 4**
Flycatcher, Brown-breasted **104: 5**
Flycatcher, Tickell's Blue **104: 6**
Garganey **77: 3**
Grebe, Little **77: 4**
Green-pigeon, Orange-breasted **88: 4**
Green-pigeon, Pompadour **88: 5**
Greenshank, Common **86: 6**
Hanging-parrot, Sri Lanka **89: 1**
Hawk-eagle, Changeable **83: 3**
Heron, Grey **80: 5**
Heron, Purple **80: 6**
Honey-buzzard, Oriental **82: 3**
Hoopoe, Eurasian **94: 6**
Hornbil, Malabar Pied **96: 1**
Hornbil, Sri Lanka Grey **96: 2**
Ibis, Black-headed **78: 4**
Imperial-pigeon, Green **88: 6**
Iora, Common **98: 2**
Jacana, Pheasant-tailed **86: 1**
Junglefowl, Sri Lanka **76: 4**

A Pictorial Guide to Uda Walawe National Park

Kestrel, Common 82: 1
Kingfisher, Black-backed 95: 4
　　　　　 Black-capped 95: 2
　　　　　 Common 95: 6
　　　　　 Pied 95: 5
　　　　　 Stork-billed 95: 1
　　　　　 White-throated 95: 3
Kite, Black-winged 82: 2
　　　 Brahminy 82: 4
Koel, Asian 91: 1
Lapwing, Red-wattled 85: 2
　　　　 Yellow-wattled 85: 1
Lark, Ashy-crowned Sparrow 100: 6
Leafbird, Golden-fronted 104: 8
　　　　 Jerdon's 104: 7
Leaf-warbler, Large-billed 101: 8
Malkoha, Blue-faced 91: 3
　　　　 Sirkeer 91: 4
　　　　 Sri Lanka Red-faced 91: 2
Minivet, Scarlet 98: 7
　　　　 Small 98: 6
Monarch, Black-naped 99: 5
Moorhen, Common 84: 4
Munia, Scaly-breasted 106: 4
　　　　 Tricoloured 106: 3
　　　　 White-rumped 106: 2
　　　　 White-throated 106: 1
Myna, Common 102: 6
　　　 Hill 102: 8
Night-heron, Black-crowned 79: 3
Nightjar, Indian 92: 5
　　　　 Jerdon's 92: 6
Nuthatch, Velvet-fronted 100: 8
Openbill, Asian 78: 2
Oriole, Black-hooded 99: 1
Owlet, Jungle 92: 4
Palm-swift, Asian 93: 2
Paradise-flycatcher, Asian 99: 4
Parakeet, Alexandrine 89: 3
　　　　 Plum-headed 89: 4
　　　　 Rose-ringed 89: 2
Peafowl, Indian 76: 5

Pelican, Spot-billed 81: 1
Pigeon, Rock 88: 1
Pipit, Paddyfield 106: 8
Pitta, Indian 96: 6
Plover, Kentish 85: 5
　　　 Lesser Sand 85: 6
　　　 Little Ringed 85: 4
　　　 Pacific Golden 85: 3
Pond-heron, Indian 79: 4
Prinia, Ashy 101: 4
　　　 Grey-breasted 101: 2
　　　 Jungle 101: 3
　　　 Plain 101: 5
Pygmy-goose, Cotton 77: 1
Quail, Blue 76: 1
Redshank, Common 86: 4
Reed-warbler, Blyth's 101: 7
Robin, Indian 104: 2
　　　 Oriental Magpie 104: 1
Roller, Indian 94: 2
Sandpiper, Common 86: 7
　　　　 Marsh 86: 3
　　　　 Wood 86: 5
Scimitar-babbler, Sri Lanka 103: 3
Scops-owl, Collared 92: 1
Sea-eagle, White-bellied 83: 2
Shama, White-rumped 104: 3
Shikra 82: 6
Shrike, Brown 98: 8
Skylark, Oriental 100: 5
Snipe, Pintail 86: 2
Sparrow, House 105: 6
Spoonbill, Eurasian 78: 3
Spurfowl, Sri Lanka 76: 3
Starling, Brahminy 102: 5
　　　　 Rosy 102: 7
Stilt, Black-winged 84: 7
Stork, Painted 78: 1
　　　 Woolly-necked 78: 6
Sunbird, Long-billed 105: 5
　　　　 Purple 105: 4
　　　　 Purple-rumped 105: 3

Swallow, Ban 93: 4
    Red-rumped 93: 6
Swamphen, Purple 84: 2
Swift, Little 93: 3
Swiftlet, Indian 93: 1
Tailorbird, Common 101: 6
Tern, Common 87: 3
    Gull-billed 87: 1
    Little 87: 4
    Roseate 87: 2
    Whiskered 87: 5
Thick-knee, Eurasian 84: 5
    Great 84: 6
Tit, Great 100: 3
Treeswift, Crested 93: 5
Trogon, Malabar 94: 1
Wagtail, Forest 106: 5
    Grey 106: 7
    Yellow 106: 6
Waterhen, White-breasted 84: 1
Weaver, Baya 105: 7
    Streaked 105: 8
Whistling-duck, Lesser 77: 2
White-eye, Oriental 100: 7
Woodpecker, Brown-capped 97: 1
    Rufous 97: 4
    Yellow-crowned 97: 2
Woodshrike, Common 98: 3
Woodswallow, Ashy 98: 1
Yellownape, Lesser 97: 3

Scientific Names

Accipiter badius 82: 6
Accipiter virgatus 82: 5
Acridotheres tristis 102: 6
Acrocephalus dumetorum 101: 7
Actitis hypoleucos 86: 7
Aegithina tiphia 98: 2
Aerodramus unicolor 93: 1
Alauda gulgula 100: 5
Alcedo atthis 95: 6
Amaurornis phoenicurus 84: 1
Anas querquedula 77: 3
Anastomus oscitans 78: 2
Anhinga melanogaster 81: 5
Anthracoceros coronatus 96: 1
Anthus rufulus 106: 8
Apus affinis 93: 3
Ardea cinerea 80: 5
Ardea purpurea 80: 6
Ardeola grayii 79: 4
Artamus fuscus 98: 1
Bubo nipalensis 92: 2
Bubulcus ibis 80: 3
Burhinus oedicnemus 84: 5
Cacomantis passerinus 90: 5
Cacomantis sonneratii 90: 4
Caprimulgus asiaticus 92: 5
Caprimulgus atripennis 92: 6
Casmerodius albus 80: 2
Celeus brachyurus 97: 4
Centropus sinensis 91: 5
Ceryle rudis 95: 5
Ceyx erithaca 95: 4
Chalcophaps indica 88: 3
Charadrius alexandrinus 85: 5
Charadrius dubius 85: 4
Charadrius mongolus 85: 6
Chlidonias hybrida 87: 5
Chloropsis aurifrons 104: 8
Chloropsis jerdoni 104: 7
Chrysocolaptes lucidus 97: 6

Chrysomma sinense **103: 5**
Ciconia episcopus **78: 6**
Cisticola juncidis **101: 1**
Clamator coromandus **90: 1**
Clamator jacobinus **90: 2**
Columba livia **88: 1**
Copsychus malabaricus **104: 3**
Copsychus saularis **104: 1**
Coracias benghalensis **94: 2**
Coracina macei **98: 4**
Coracina melanoptera **98: 5**
Corvus levaillantii **100: 1**
Corvus splendens **100: 2**
Coturnix chinensis **76: 1**
Cuculus micropterus **90: 3**
Cyornis tickelliae **104: 6**
Cypsiurus balasiensis **93: 2**
Dendrocopos mahrattensis **97: 2**
Dendrocopos nanus **97: 1**
Dendrocygna javanica **77: 2**
Dendronanthus indicus **106: 5**
Dicaeum agile **105: 1**
Dicaeum erythrorhynchos **105: 2**
Dicrurus caerulescens **99: 2**
Dicrurus paradiseus **99: 3**
Dinopium benghalense **97: 5**
Ducula aenea **88: 6**
Dumetia hyperythra **103: 2**
Egretta garzetta **80: 4**
Elanus caeruleus **82: 2**
Eremopterix griseus **100: 6**
Esacus recurvirostris **84: 6**
Eudynamys scolopaceus **91: 1**
Falco tinnunculus **82: 1**
Fulica atra **84: 3**
Gallinago stenura **86: 2**
Gallinula chloropus **84: 4**
Galloperdix bicalcarata **76: 3**
Gallus lafayetii **76: 4**
Glaucidium radiatum **92: 4**
Gracula religiosa **102: 8**
Halcyon pileata **95: 2**

Halcyon smyrnensis **95: 3**
Haliaeetus leucogaster **83: 2**
Haliastur indus **82: 4**
Harpactes fasciatus **94: 1**
Hemiprocne coronata **93: 5**
Himantopus himantopus **84: 7**
Hirundo daurica **93: 6**
Hirundo rustica **93: 4**
Hydrophasianus chirurgus **86: 1**
Hypothymis azurea **99: 5**
Hypsipetes leucocephalus **102: 4**
Ichthyophaga ichthyaetus **83: 1**
Ixobrychus cinnamomeus **79: 1**
Ixobrychus flavicollis **79: 5**
Ixobrychus sinensis **79: 2**
Ketupa zeylonensis **92: 3**
Lanius cristatus **98: 8**
Leptoptilos javanicus **78: 5**
Lonchura malabarica **106: 1**
Lonchura malacca **106: 3**
Lonchura punctulata **106: 4**
Lonchura striata **106: 2**
Loriculus beryllinus **89: 1**
Megalaima haemacephala **96: 4**
Megalaima rubricapillus **96: 5**
Megalaima zeylanica **96: 3**
Merops leschenaulti **94: 5**
Merops orientalis **94: 4**
Merops philippinus **94: 3**
Mesophoyx intermedia **80: 1**
Mirafra affinis **100: 4**
Motacilla cinerea **106: 7**
Motacilla flava **106: 6**
Muscicapa daurica **104: 4**
Muscicapa muttui **104: 5**
Mycteria leucocephala **78: 1**
Nectarinia asiatica **105: 4**
Nectarinia lotenia **105: 5**
Nectarinia zeylonica **105: 3**
Nettapus coromandelianus **77: 1**
Nycticorax nycticorax **79: 3**
Ocyceros gingalensis **96: 2**

Oriolus xanthornus **99: 1**
Orthotomus sutorius **101: 6**
Otus bakkamoena **92: 1**
Parus cinereus **100: 3**
Passer domesticus **105: 6**
Pavo cristatus **76: 5**
Pelargopsis capensis **95: 1**
Pelecanus philippensis **81: 1**
Pellorneum fuscocapillus **103: 1**
Pericrocotus cinnamomeus **98: 6**
Pericrocotus flammeus **98: 7**
Pernis ptilorhyncus **82: 3**
Phaenicophaeus leschenaultii **91: 4**
Phaenicophaeus pyrrhocephalus **91: 2**
Phaenicophaeus viridirostris **91: 3**
Phalacrocorax carbo **81: 4**
Phalacrocorax fuscicollis **81: 3**
Phalacrocorax niger **81: 2**
Phylloscopus magnirostris **101: 8**
Picus chlorolophus **97: 3**
Pitta brachyura **96: 6**
Platalea leucorodia **78: 3**
Ploceus manyar **105: 8**
Ploceus philippinus **105: 7**
Pluvialis fulva **85: 3**
Pomatorhinus melanurus **103: 3**
Porphyrio porphyrio **84: 2**
Prinia hodgsonii **101: 2**
Prinia inornata **101: 5**
Prinia socialis **101: 4**
Prinia sylvatica **101: 3**
Psittacula cyanocephala **89: 4**
Psittacula eupatria **89: 3**
Psittacula krameri **89: 2**
Pycnonotus cafer **102: 3**
Pycnonotus luteolus **102: 2**
Pycnonotus melanicterus **102: 1**
Rhipidura aureola **99: 6**
Rhopocichla atriceps **103: 4**
Saxicoloides fulicatus **104: 2**
Sitta frontalis **100: 8**
Spilornis cheela **83: 4**

Spizaetus cirrhatus **83: 3**
Sterna albifrons **87: 4**
Sterna dougallii **87: 2**
Sterna hirundo **87: 3**
Sterna nilotica **87: 1**
Stigmatopelia chinensis **88: 2**
Sturnus pagodarum **102: 5**
Sturnus roseus **102: 7**
Surniculus lugubris **90: 6**
Tachybaptus ruficollis **77: 4**
Tephrodornis pondicerianus **98: 3**
Terpsiphone paradisi **99: 4**
Threskiornis melanocephalus **78: 4**
Treron bicinctus **88: 4**
Treron pompadora **88: 5**
Tringa glareola **86: 5**
Tringa nebularia **86: 6**
Tringa stagnatilis **86: 3**
Tringa totanus **86: 4**
Turdoides affinis **103: 6**
Turnix suscitator **76: 2**
Upupa epops **94: 6**
Vanellus indicus **85: 2**
Vanellus malabaricus **85: 1**
Zosterops palpebrosus **100: 7**

Index of Mammals

Numbers refer to plate numbers and illustration numbers, not page numbers.

Common Names

Bat, Bicoloured Leaf-nosed **107: 2**
    Black-bearded Sheath-tailed **107: 1**
    Fulvous Fruit **108: 2**
    Painted **108: 5**
    Rufous Horse-shoe **108: 3**
    Schneider's Leaf-nosed **107: 3**
    Short-nosed Fruit **107: 4**
Boar, Wild **112: 3**
Buffalo, Wild **111: 5**
Cat, Jungle **110: 1**
Civet, Common Palm **111: 2**
    Ring-tailed **111: 3**
Deer, Spotted **112: 1**
    Sri Lanka Mouse **112: 4**
Elephant, Asian **111: 4**
Fox, Indian Flying **108: 1**
Gerbil, Indian **114: 4**
Hare, Black-naped **115: 3**
Jackal, Golden **109: 6**
Langur, Grey **109: 3**
Leopard **110: 2**
Loris, Sri Lanka Red Slender **109: 4**
Macaque, Sri Lanka Toque **109: 2**
Metad, Soft-furred **113: 2**
Mongoose, Ruddy **110: 5**
    Brown **110: 3**
    Striped-neck **110: 4**
Monkey, Sri Lanka Purple-faced Leaf **109: 1**
Mouse, Asiatic Long-tailed
    Climbing **114: 3**
    Indian Field **113: 4**
    Indian House **114: 1**
    Sri Lanka Spiny **113: 5**
Otter **111: 1**
Pangolin **109: 5**
Pipistrelle, Pygmy **108: 4**
Porcupine **112: 2**
Rat, Black **114: 2**
    White-tailed **113: 3**
Sambhur **112: 5**
Shrew, Common Musk **113: 1**
Squirrel, Sri Lanka Giant **115: 2**
    Palm **115: 1**

Scientific Names

Axis axis **112: 1**
Bubalus arnee **111: 5**
Canis aureus **109: 6**
Cervus unicolor **112: 5**
Cynopterus sphinx **107: 4**
Elephas maximus **111: 4**
Felis chaus **110: 1**
Funambulus palmarum **115: 1**
Herpestes fuscus **110: 3**
Herpestes smithii **110: 5**
Herpestes vitticollis **110: 4**
Hipposideros ater **107: 2**
Hipposideros speoris **107: 3**
Hystrix indica **112: 2**
Kerivoula picta **108: 5**
Lepus nigricollis **115: 3**
Loris tardigradus **109: 4**
Lutra lutra **111: 1**
Macaca sinica **109: 2**
Madromys blanfordi **113: 3**
Manis crassicaudata **109: 5**
Millardia meltada **113: 2**
Moschiola meminna **112: 4**
Mus booduga **113: 4**
Mus fernandoni **113: 5**
Mus musculus **114: 1**
Panthera pardus **110: 2**
Paradoxurus hermaphoditus **111: 2**
Pipistrellus tenuis **108: 4**
Pteropus giganteus **108: 1**
Rattufa macroura **115: 2**
Rattus rattus **114: 2**
Rhinolophus rouxii **108: 3**
Rousettus leschenaulti **108: 2**
Semnopithecus priam **109: 3**
Semnopithecus vetulus **109: 1**
Suncus murinus **113: 1**
Sus scrofa **112: 3**
Taphozous melanopogon **107: 1**
Tatera indica **114: 4**
Vendeleuria oleracea **114: 3**
Viverricula indica **111: 3**

Checklists

Checklist of Plants

No	Scientific Name	Common Name
Family- **Acanthaceae**		
01	*Barleria prionitis*	Porcupine flower / කටු කරද, කටු කරඩු
Family- **Acanthaceae**		
02	*Stenosiphonium cordifolium*	ඩු නෙළු, නෙළු
Family- **Amaryllidaceae**		
03	*Crinum defixum*	හීන් තොලබෝ
Family- **Anacardiaceae**		
04	*Mangifera zeylanica*	ඇටඹ, වල් අඹ
Family- **Annonaceae**		
05	*Miliusa indica*	කැකිලි-මැස්ස
06	*Polyalthia korinti*	මී වැන්න, උල් කෙන්ද
Family- **Apocynaceae**		
07	*Carissa spinarum*	හීන් කරඹ
Family- **Arecaceae**		
08	*Phoenix pusilla*	ඉඳි
Family- **Asclepiadaceae**		
09	*Calotropis gigantea*	එළ වරා, හෙළ වරා, වරා
10	*Wattakaka volubilis*	Green Milkweed climber / අඟුණ, අනුක්කෝල, තිරි අඟුණ, තිත්ත අඟුණ
Family- **Asteraceae**		
11	*Eupatorium odoratum*	
Family- **Bignoniaceae**		
12	*Stereospermum colais*	ලුණු මඬල, දුනු මඬල
Family- **Boraginaceae**		
13	*Carmona retusa*	හීන් තඹල
14	*Ehretia laevis*	
Family- **Capparaceae**		
15	*Capparis Zeylanica*	සුදු වෙලන්ගිරිය
16	*Crateva adansonii*	Garlic pear tree / ලුණු වරණ
Family- **Colchicaceae**		
17	*Gloriosa superba*	නියඟලා
Family- **Combretaceae**		
18	*Terminalia arjuna*	කුඹුක්, කුඹුළු

No	Scientific Name	Common Name	
Family- **Connaraceae**			
19	*Connarus monocarpus*	රදලීය	
Family- **Convolvulaceae**			
20	*Argyreia osyrensis*	දුම්බඳ	
Family- **Dilleniaceae**			
21	*Dillenia indica*	හොඳපර, වම්පර	
Family- **Dipterocarpaceae**			
22	*Hopea cordifolia*	මෙන්දෝර, උඩ මෙන්දෝර	
Family- **Ebenaceae**			
23	*Diospyros ebenum*	Ebony / කළුවර	
24	*Diospyros montana*		
25	*Diospyros ovalifolia*	හබර, කුණුමැල්ල	
26	*Maba buxifolia*		
Family- **Erythroxylaceae**			
	Erythroxylum zeylanicum		
Family- **Euphorbiaceae**			
27	*Bridelia retusa*	කැටකෑල	
28	*Dimorphocalyx glabellus*	වැලිවැන්න	
29	*Drypetes sepiaria*	වීර	
30	*Euphorbia antiquorum*	දළුක්	
31	*Flueggea leucopyrus*	Bushweed / හීන් කටුපිල	
32	*Phyllanthus polyphyllus*	කුරටිය	
Family- **Fabaceae**			
33	*Acacia leucophloea*	කටු අන්දර, මහ අන්දර	
34	*Bauhinia racemosa*	මයිල	
35	*Bauhinia tomentosa*	කහ පෙතන්, පෙතන්	
36	*Cassia auriculata*	රණවරා	
37	*Cassia roxburghii*	Red cassia / රතු වා	
38	*Crotalaria spp.*	අඩන-හිරියා	
39	*Derris parviflora*	කළ වැල්, සුදු කළ වැල්	
40	*Derris scandens*	අල වැල්, බෝ කළ වැල්, කළ වැල්	
41	*Dichrostachys cinerea*	Bell mimosa / අන්දර	
42	*Pongamia pinnata*	Indian beech, Mullikulam tree / ගල් කරඳ, කරඳ, මගුල් කරඳ	
43	*Tamarindus indica*	Tamarind / සියඹලා, මහ සියඹලා	
44	*Uraria picta*		

No	Scientific Name	Common Name	
Family- **Hippocrataceae**			
45	*Salacia reticulata*	කොතල හිඹුටු, හිඹුට වැල්	
Family- **Lauraceae**			
46	*Alseodaphne semecarpifolia*	වෑවරණ	
Family- **Linaceae**			
47	*Hugonia mystax*	බූ ගැටිය, මහ ගැටිය, වටිටි වැටි	
Family- **Loganiaceae**			
48	*Strychnos nux-vomica*	Nux vomica / ගොඩ කදුරු	
49	*Strychnos potatorum*	Clearing-nut / ඉඟිණ	
50	*Dendrophthoe falcata*	පිළිල	
Family- **Malvaceae**			
51	*Hibiscus micranthus*	බැබිල	
Family- **Melastomataceae**			
52	*Memecylon angustifolium*	Blue mist / කොර කහ	
53	*Memecylon umbellatum*	Blue mist / කොර කහ	
Family- **Meliaceae**			
54	*Azadirachta indica*	Margosa Neem / කොහොඹ	
55	*Walsura trifoliolata*	කිරිකෝන්, මල්පෙත්ත	
Family- **Moraceae**			
56	*Ficus benghalensis*	Banyan / මහ නුග	
57	*Streblus asper*	Crooked rough-bush / ගැට නෙටුල්	
58	*Streblus taxoides*	Fig-lime / ගොන් ගොටු	
Family- **Myrtaceae**			
59	*Eucalyptus spp.*		
60	*Eugenia bracteata*	තැඹිලිය	
61	*Syzygium cumini*	මා දං, මහ දං	
Family- **Ochnaceae**			
62	*Ochna lanceolata*	බෝ කෑර, මල් කෑර	
63	*Jasminum auriculatum*		
Family- **Poaceae**			
64	*Panicum maximum*	Guinea grass / රට තණ	
Family- **Rhamnaceae**			
65	*Scutia myrtina*		
66	*Ventilago madraspatana*	යකා වැල්, යකඩ වැල්	
67	*Ziziphus oenoplia*	හීන එරමිණියා	

No	Scientific Name	Common Name	
Family- Rubiaceae			
68	*Benkara malabarica*	පුදන්	
69	*Canthium coromandelicum*	කර	
70	*Catunaregam spinosa*	කුකුර්මාන්, කුකුරුමාන්	
71	*Haldina cordifolia*	කොලොන්	
72	*Mitragyna parviflolia*	හැලඹ	
73	*Morinda coreia*	අහු	
74	*Mussaenda frondosa*	මුස්සැණ්ඩා, මුස්වැන්න, වෙල් බුත්සරණ	
75	*Tarenna asiatica*	තරණ	
Family- Rutaceae			
76	*Atalantia monophylla*		
77	*Chloroxylon swietenia*	Satinwood / බුරුත	
78	*Clausena indica*	මී ගොන් කරපිංචා	
79	*Glycosmis mauritiana*		
80	*Limonia acidissima*	Elephant-apple, Woodapple / දිවුල්	
81	*Murraya paniculata*	Orange jessamine / ඇටිටේරියා	
82	*Paramignya monophylla*	වෙල්ලන්ගිරිය	
83	*Pleiospermium alatum*	තුම්පත් කුරුදු, තුන්පත් කුරුදු	
84	*Toddalia asiatica*	කුඩු-මිරිස්	
Family- Sapindaceae			
85	*Lepisanthes tetraphylla*		
86	*Sapindus emarginata*	Soap nut tree / පෙනෙල, කහ පෙනෙල	
87	*Schleichera oleosa*	Ceylon oak / කෝන්	
Family- Sapotaceae			
88	*Manilkara hexandra*	පලු	
Family- Sterculiaceae			
89	*Pterospermum suberifolium*	Fishing rod tree / වෙලන්, වෙලන්ගු, වෙලුන්	
Family- Tiliaceae			
90	*Grewia damine*	දම්මිණය	
91	*Grewia orientalis*	වැල් කෙලිය, වැල් මැදිය	
Family- Ulmaceae			
92	*Holoptelea integrifolia*	Indian Elm / ගොඩ කිරිල්ල	

No	Scientific Name	Common Name	1
Family- **Verbenaceae**			
93	*Gmelina asiatica*	Asiatic beechberry / දෙමට, ගැට දෙමට	
94	*Lantana camara*	ගඳපාන, ගර්දපාන, ගෙදපාන, කටු හිඟුරු, ටොන්කිසද්ඳ	
95	*Premna tomentosa*	බූ සයිරු ගස්, බූ සේරු, නු සයිරු	
96	*Tectona grandis*	Indian oak, Teak / තේක්ක	
97	*Vitex altissima*	මිල්ල	
98	*Vitex negundo*	Chaste Tree / හෙලරික, නික, නිල් නික, සුදු නික, නිර්ගුණ්ඩි	
Family- **Vitaceae**			
99	*Cissus quadrangularis*	හිරැස්ස, සිරැස්ස	
100	*Cissus vitiginea*	වල් නිවිති	

Checklist of Molluscs

No	Scientific Name	Common Name	1
MOLLUSCS			
<u>Opperculate Gastrapods</u>			
01	*Paludomus zeylanica*		
02	*Bellamya ceylonica*		
03	*Pila globosa*		
04	*Melanoides tuberculata*		
05	*Indoplanorbis exustus*		
06	*Lymnaea pinguis*		
07	*Bithynia inconspicus*		
<u>Bivalve Molluscs</u>			
08	*Lamellidens marginalis*		
LAND SNAILS			
09	*Beddomea trifasciatus* (Lowland form)		
10	*Euplecta* spp.		
11	*Rhachistia pulcher*		
12	*Mirus panos*		
13	*Eurychlamys vilipensa*		
14	*Cryptozona bistrialis*		
15	*Aulopoma itieri* var. *hofmeisteri*		
16	*Pterocyclus troscheli*		
17	*Theobaldius* spp.		
18	*Micraulax coeloconus*		

Checklist of Arthropoda

No	Scientific Name	Common Name	1
	AQUATIC ARTHROPODS		
Water Bugs			
01	*Lethocerus indicus*		
02	*Sphaeroderma rusticum*		
Whirlygig Beetles			
03	*Gyrinus* spp.		
Back Swimmers / Boatman			
04	*Anisops barbata*		
Diving Beetles			
05	*Cybister* spp.		
Digging Beetles			
06	*Hydrocoptus* spp.		
Water Scorpion			
07	*Laccotrephes grossus*		
Water Striders			
08	*Gerris adelaidis*		
Water Stick Insect			
09	*Ranatra filiformis*		
Fresh water Lobster			
10	*Macrobrachium rosenbergii*		
Fresh water Crab			
11	*Parathelpheus spps; Ceylonothalpheus* spp, etc		
	INSECT LARVAE		
12	*Trichoptera* (Caddisfly) Larvae		
13	*Anophiline* (Mosquito) Larvae		
14	*Neuroptera* (Alderfly) Larvae		
15	*Odonata* (Damselfly) Larvae		
16	*Odonata* (Dragonfly) Larvae		
17	*Cybister* (Water Beetle) Larvae		
18	*Odonata* (Mayfly) Larvae		

No	Scientific Name	Common Name	1
TERSTRIAL ARTHROPODS - I			
19	*Tethigonia* spp.	Grasshoppers	
20	*Dysdercus ungulates*		
21	*Luciola* spp.	Fire Flies	
22	*Mantis* spp.	Praying Mantis	
23	*Acheta* spp.	Cricket	
24	*Tibicen* spp.	Cicarda	
25	*Coccinella* spp.	Lady bird Beetles	
26	*Forficula* spp.	Earwig	
27	*Blatta* spp.	Coackoroach	
28	*Gyroptalpa* spp.	Mole Ant	
TERSTRIAL ARTHROPODS - II			
29	*Scolopander* spp.	Centipedes	
30	Millipedes	*Julis* spp. - Small	
31		Millipede - Medium	
32		Millipede - Long	
33	*Distoleon tetragrammicus*	Ant Fly	
34	*Luciola* spp.	Fire Fly	
35	*Rhipicephalus microplus*	Cattle Ticks	
36	*Heterometrus swarmmerdami*	Scoprion	
BEES, WASPS & HORNETS			
37	*Apis cerena*	Honey Bee / මීමැස්සා	
38	*Apis dorsata*	Rock Honey Bee / බමඹරා	
39	*Apis florae*	Dwarf Honey Bee / දඩුවැල් මීමැස්සා	
40	*Trigona iridipennis*	Stingless Honey Bee / කණෙයියා	
41	*Xylocopa tenuiscapa*	Gaint Carpenter Bee / අම්ඹලන් පාළුවා	
42	*Vespa orientalis*	Hornet / දෙඹරා	
43	*Eumenes coarctatus*	Potter wasp / කුඹලා	

Checklist of Dung Beetles

No	Scientific Name	Common Name	1
Family- **Scarabaeinae**			
01	*Paragymnopleurus koenegi*		
02	*Copris signatus*		
03	*Catharsius molossus*		
04	*Copris sodalis*		
05	*Onthophagus gazella*		
06	*Onthophagus difficilis*		
07	*Onthophagus militaris*		
08	*Onthophagus spinifex*		
09	*Onthophagus unifasciatus*		
10	*Paragymnopleurus melanarius*		

Checklist of Spiders

No	Scientific Name	Common Name	
Family- **Theraphosidae**			
01	*Poecilotheria pederseni*	Sri Lanka Pederseni's Tiger Spider / ශ්‍රී ලංකා පෙඩර්සර්න්ගේ දිවි මකුළුවා	
Family- **Hersiliidae**			
02	*Hersilia savignyi*	Common Two-tailed spider / හර්සිලියා මකුළුවා / පොදු දෙනැටි මකුළුවා	
Family- **Theridiidae**			
03	*Argyrodes flavescens*	Red and silver Dewdrop Spider / රතු රිදී පිණිබිඳු මකුළුවා	
Family- **Tetragnathidae**			
04	*Tetragnatha viridorufa*	Common Long-jawed Orbweaver / පොදු දිගු හනුක දිය මකුළුවා	
Family- **Nephilidae**			
05	*Herennia multipuncta*	Ornate Tree trunk Spider / ආසියා විසිතුරු පැතලි මකුළුවා	
06	*Nephila pilipes*	Giant Wood Spider / යෝධ වන මකුළුවා	
Family- **Araneidae**			
07	*Neoscona nautica*	Brown Sailor Spider / පොදු ගෙවතු මකුළුවා	
08	*Gasteracantha geminata*	Common Kite Spider / Common Spiny-orb Weaver / පොදු සරංගල් මකුළුවා	
09	*Argiope anasuja*	Signature Spider / ලියන දැල් වියන්නා	
10	*Nephilengys malabarensis*	Hermit Spider / පොදු වෙරම් නිවෙස් මකුළුවා	
Family- **Lycosidae**			
11	*Hippasa greenalliae*	Grass Funnel-web Spider / විදුලි බිම් හමන්නා	
Family- **Pisauridae**			
12	*Dolomedes (cf.) triton*	Six-spotted Fishing Spider / තිත් සයැති දිය මකුළුවා	
Family- **Oxopidae**			
13	*Oxyopes macilentus*	Yellow-striped Lynx Spider / කහ ඉරි ලින්ක්ස් මකුළුවා	
Family- **Agelenidae**			
14	*Tegenaria domestica*	Grass Funnel-weaver / කේතු දැල් වියන්නා	

No	Scientific Name	Common Name	
Family- **Sparassidae**			
15	*Heteropoda venatoria*	Domestic Huntsman Spider / පුළුන් කොට්ටා මකුළුවා	
Family- **Thomisidae**			
16	*Oxytate subvirens*	Sri Lanka Elongated Green Crab Spider / ශ්‍රී ලංකා කොළ කකුළු මකුළුවා	
17	*Thomisus spectabilis*	White Flower Crab Spider / ඇලි කකුළු මකුළුවා	
Family- **Salticidae**			
18	*Phintella vittata*	Banded Phintella / කුරු පිනුම් මකුළුවා	
19	*Plexippus petersi*	Common House Fly Catcher / මකුළු මැසිමාරා	
20	*Siler semiglaucus*	Red & blue Tiny Jumper / නිල් විසිතුරු පිනුම් මකුළුවා	
21	*Myrmarachne maxillosea*	Giant Ant-like Jumper / කළු කඩි මකුළුවා	
22	*Myrmarachne palataleoides*	Red Ant-like Jumper / දිමි මකුළුවා	
23	*Telamonia dimidiata*	Two-striped Telamonia / යෝධ දෙඉරි පිනුම් මකුළුවා	

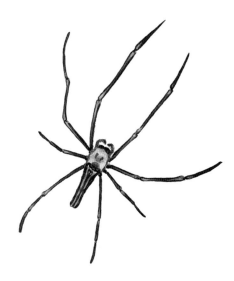

Checklist of Dragonflies & Damselflies

No	Scientific Name	Common Name	
Family- **Chlorocyphidae**			
01	*Libellago greeni*	Green's Gem	
02	*Libellago finalis*	Ultima Gem	
Family- **Coenagrionidae**			
03	*Ischnura senegalensis*	Common Bluetail	
04	*Pseudagrion malabaricum*	Malabar Sprite	
05	*Pseudagrion rubriceps*	Orange-faced Sprite	
06	*Agriocnemis pygmaea*	Wandering Wisp	
07	*Ceriagrion coromandelianum*	Yellow Waxtail	
Family- **Gomphidae**			
08	*Ichtinogomphus rapax*	Rapacious Flangetail	
Family- **Libellulidae**			
09	*Brachythemis contaminata*	Asian Groundling	
10	*Acisoma panorpoides*	Asian Pintail	
11	*Diplacodes nebulosa*	Black-tipped Percher	
12	*Diplacodes trivialis*	Blue Percher	
13	*Potamarcha congener*	Blue Persuer	
14	*Trithemis aurora*	Crimson Dropwing	
15	*Trithemis pallidinervis*	Dancing Dropwing	
16	*Orthetrum sabina*	Green Skimmer	
17	*Bradinopyga geminata*	Indian Rockdweller	
18	*Crocothemis servilia*	Oriental Scarlet	
19	*Neurothemis tullia*	Pied Parasol	
20	*Orthetrum pruinosum*	Pink Skimmer	
21	*Urothemis signata*	Scarlet Basker	
22	*Tramea limbata*	Sociable Glider	
23	*Rhyothemis variegata*	Variegated Flutterer	
24	*Pantala flavescens*	Wandering Glider	
Family- **Platycnemididae**			
25	*Copera marginipes*	Yellow Featherleg	

Checklist of Butterflies

No	Common Name	Scientific Name	1
Family- **Papilionidae**			
01	*Troides darsius*	Sri Lanka Birdwing	
02	*Pachiopta hector*	Crimson Rose	
03	*Pachliopta aristolochiae*	Common Rose	
04	*Papilio crino*	Banded Peacock	
05	*Papilio demoleus*	Lime Butterfly	
06	*Papilio polymnestor*	Blue Mormon	
07	*Chilasa clytia*	Mine	
Family- **Pieridae**			
08	*Leptosia nina*	Psyche	
09	*Delias eucharis*	Jezebel	
10	*Belenois aurota*	Pioneer	
11	*Cepora nerissa*	Common Gull	
12	*Appias albina*	Common Albatross	
13	*Lxias marianne*	White Orange-tip	
14	*Hebomoia glaucippe*	Great Orange-tip	
15	*Catopsilia pyranthe*	Mottled Immigrant	
16	*Pareronia ceylanica*	Dark Wanderer	
17	*Colotis amata*	Small Salmon-arab	
18	*Colotis etrida*	Little Orange-tip	
19	*Eurema brigitta*	Small Grass-yellow	
20	*Eurema hecabe*	Common Grass-yellow	
21	*Eurema blanda*	Three-spot Grass-yellow	
Family- **Danaidae**			
22	*Idea iasonia*	Tree Nymph	
23	*Parantica aglea*	Glassy Tiger	
24	*Danaus chrysippus*	Plain Tiger	
25	*Euploea core*	Common Crow	
Family- **Nymphalidae**			
26	*Ariadne ariadne*	Angled Castor	
27	*Cupha erymanthis*	Rustic	
28	*Phalanta phalantha*	Leopard	
29	*Vindula erota*	Cruiser	

No	Common Name	Scientific Name	
30	*Cirrochroa thais*	Tamil Yeoman	
31	*Cethosia nietneri*	Lace Wing	
32	*Vanessa cardui*	Painted Lady	
33	*Junonia atlites*	Grey Pansy	
34	*Junonia almana*	Peacock Pansy	
35	*Hypolimnas misippus*	Danaid Eggfly	
36	*Kallima philarchus*	Sri Lanka Blue Oakleaf	
37	*Neptis hylas*	Common Sailor	
38	*Neptis jumbah*	Chestnut-streaked Sailor	
39	*Moduza procris*	Commander	
40	*Parthenos sylvia*	Clipper	
41	*Euthalia aconthea*	Baron	
42	*Rohana parisatis*	Black Prince	
43	*Polyura athamas*	Nawab	
44	*Charaxes psaphon*	Tawny Rajah	

Family- **Acraeidae**

No	Common Name	Scientific Name	
45	*Acraeu violae*	Tawny Coster	

Family- **Satyridae**

No	Common Name	Scientific Name	
46	*Melannitis leda*	Common Eveningbrown	
47	*Lethe rohria*	Common Treebrown	
48	*Orsotriaena medus*	Nigger	
49	*Mycalesis perseus*	Common Bushbrown	
50	*Ypthima ceylonica*	White Four-ring	
51	*Elymnias hypermnestra*	Common Plamfly	

Family- **Lycaenidae**

No	Common Name	Scientific Name	
52	*Spalgis epeus*	Apefly	
53	*Curetis thetis*	Indian Sunbeam	
54	*Arhopala pseudocentaurus*	Centaur Oakblue	
55	*Surendra vivarna*	Common Acaciablue	
56	*Zesius chrysomallus*	Redspot	
57	*Amblypodia anita*	Purple Leafblue	
58	*Catapaecilma major*	Common Tinsel	
59	*Loxura atymnus*	Yamfly	
60	*Rathinda amor*	Monkey Puzzle	
61	*Cheritra freja*	Common Imperial	
62	*Spindasis vulcanus*	Common Silverline	
63	*Hypolycaena nilgirica*	Nilgiri Tit	

No	Common Name	Scientific Name	
64	Bindahara phocides	Plane	
65	Virachola isocrates	Common Guavablue	
66	Deudorix epijarbas	Cornelian	
67	Anthene lycaenina	Pointed Ciliateblue	
68	Petrelaea dana	Dingy Lineblue	
69	Nacaduba sinhala	Sri Lanka Pale 6-Lineblue	
70	Prosotas nora	Common Lineblue	
71	Jamides bochus	Dark Cerulean	
72	Jamides alecto	Metallic Cerulean	
73	Jamides celeno	Common Cerulean	
74	Catochrysops strabo	Forget-me-not	
75	Lampides boeticus	Pea Blue	
76	Synatarucus plinius	Zebra Blue	
77	Castalius rosimon	Common Pierrot	
78	Freyeria trochilus	Grass Jewel	
79	Zizina otis	Lesser Grassblue	
80	Zizula hylax	Tiny Grassblue	
81	Talicada nyseus	Red Pierrot	
82	Everes lacturnus	Indian Cupid	
83	Actyolepis puspa felderi	Common Hedgeblue	
84	Neopithicops zalmora	Quaker	
85	Megisba malaya	Malayan	
86	Euchrysops cnejus	Gram Blue	
87	Chilades lajus	Lime Blue	

Family- **Riodinidae**

No	Common Name	Scientific Name	
88	Abisara echerius	Plum Judy	

Family- **Hesperiidae** (Skippers, Darters & Flats)

No	Common Name	Scientific Name	
89	Bibasis oedipodea ataphus	Branded orange Awlet	
90	Badamia exclamationis	Brown Awl	
91	Gangara thyrsis clothilda	Giant Redeye	
92	Celaenorrhinus spilothyrus	Sri Lanka Black Flat	
93	Coladenia indrani	Tricolour Pied Flat	
94	Sarangesa dasahara aibicilia	Common Small Flat	
95	Tagiades japetus obscurus	Ceylon Snow Flat	
96	Caprona ransonnettii ransonnettii	Golden Angle	
97	Amittia dioscorides singa	Bush Hopper	
98	Suastus gremius subgrisea	Indian palm Bob	

No	Common Name	Scientific Name	1
99	*Iambrix salsala luteipalpus*	Chestnt Bob	
100	*Notocrypta paralysos alysia*	Common Banded Demon	
101	*Hyarotis adrastus*	Tree Flitter	
102	*Matapa aria*	Common Redeye	
103	*Spalia galba*	Indian Skipper	
104	*Taractrocera maevius*	Common Grassdart	
105	*Oriens goloides*	Common Dartlet	
106	*Potanthus confuscius satra*	Tropic Dart	
107	*Telicota colon amba*	Pale Palmdart	
108	*Pelopidas conjuncta narooa*	Conjoined Swift	
109	*Parnara bada bada*	Smallest Swift	

Checklist of Fishes

No	Scientific Name	Common Name	
Family- **Cyprinidae**			
01	*Amblypharyngodon melettinus*	Silver Carplet / සොරයා	
02	*Catla catla*	Catla / කැටලා	
03	*Cirrhinus mrigala*	Mrigal / මිරිගල	
04	*Ctenopharyngodon idella*	Grass Carp / තණකොළ කාපයා	
05	*Devario malabaricus*	Giant Danio / රත් කයිලයා හෝ දම්කොල සාලයා	
06	*Esomus thernoicos*	Sri Lanka Flying Barb / ශ්‍රී ලංකා රැවුල් දණ්ඩියා	
07	*Garra ceylonensis*	Sri Lanka Stone Sucker / ශ්‍රී ලංකා ගල් පාඩියා	
08	*Labeo dussumieri*	Common Labeo / හිරි කනයා	
09	*Labeo rohita*	Rohu / රොහු	
10	*Puntius bimaculatus*	Redside Barb / ඉපිලි කඩයා	
11	*Puntius thermalis*	Sri Lanka Swamp Barb / ශ්‍රී ලංකා කොට පෙතියා	
12	*Puntius dorsalis*	Long-snouted Barbb / කටු පෙතියා	
13	*Systomus timbiri*	Sri Lanka Olive Barb / ශ්‍රී ලංකා මස් පෙතියා	
14	*Dawkinsia sinhala*	Sri lanka Filamented Barb / ශ්‍රී ලංකා දම්කොල පෙතියා	
15	*Puntius vittatus*	Silver Barb / බණ්ඩි තිත්තයා	
16	*Rasbora microchephala*	Stripped Rasbora / කිරි දණ්ඩියා	
17	*Tor khudree*	Mehseer / ලෙහෙල්ලා	
Family- **Siluridac**			
18	*Ompok bimaculatus*	Butter Catfish / වලපොත්තා	
Family- **Bagridac**			
19	*Mystus vittatus*	Striped Dwarf Catfish / ඉරි අංකුට්ටා	
Family- **Heteropnenstidac**			
20	*Heteropneustes fossilis*	Stinging Catfish / හුංගා	
Family- **Cichlidac**			
21	*Etroplus maculatus*	Orange Chromide / කහ කොරලියා	
22	*Etroplus suratensis*	Pearl Spot / කොරලියා	
23	*Oreochromis niloticus*	Tilapia / තිලාපියා	

No	Scientific Name	Common Name	1
24	*Oreochromis mossambicus*	Tilapia / තිලාපියා, තෙත්පිලියා, ජපන් බට්ටා හෝ බට්ටා	
Family- **Gobiidac**			
25	*Glossogobius giuris*	Bar eyed Goby / මහ වැලිගොච්චා	
Family- **Osphronemidae**			
26	*Osphronemus goramy*	Giant Gourami / සෙප්පිලි, තිත්පිලියා හෝ යෝධ ගුරාමියා	
Family- **Hemiramphidac**			
27	*Zenarchopterus dispar*	Halfbeak / මොරැල්ලා	
Family- **Synbranchidac**			
28	*Chamma gachua*	Brown Snakehead / පරඬැල් කනයා	
29	*Channa punctata*	Spotted Snakehead / මඩ කනයා	
30	*Channa striata*	Murrel / ලූලා	

Checklist of Amphibians

No	Scientific Name	Common Name	1
Family- **Bufonidae**			
01	*Duttaphrynus melanostictus*	Common Toad / ගෙයි ගෙම්බා	
Family- **Dicroglossidae**			
02	*Euphlyctis cyanophlyctis*	Indian Skipper Frog / උත්පතන මැඩියා	
03	*Euphlyctis hexadactylus*	Six-toe Green Frog / සයැඟිලි පලා මැඩියා	
04	*Hoplobatrachus crassus*	Jerdon's Bull Frog / ජඩන්ගේ දිය මැඩියා	
05	*Fejervarya limnocharis*	Common Paddyfield Frog / වෙල් මැඩියා	
Family- **Microhylidae**			
06	*Kaloula taprobanica*	Common Bull frog / විසිතුරු රතු මැඩියා	
07	*Microhyla ornata*	Ornate Narrow-mouth Frog / විසිතුරු මුව පටු මැඩියා	
08	*Microhyla rubra*	Red narrow Mouth frog / රතු මුව පටු මැඩියා	
09	*Ramanella variegata*	White-bellied Pug-snout Frog / බඩ සුදු මොට හොඹු මැඩියා	
Family- **Ranidae**			
10	*Haylarana gracilis*	Sri Lanka Wood frog / ශ්‍රී ලංකා දිය මැඩියා	
Family- **Rhacophoridae**			
11	*Polypedates cruciger*	Common Hour-glass Tree frog / සුලබ පහිඹු ගස් මැඩියා	
12	*Polypedates maculatus*	Spotted Tree frog / පුල්ලි ගස් මැඩියා	

Checklist of Reptiles

No	Scientific Name	Common Name	
Family- **Boidae**			
01	*Python molurus*	Rock Python / පිඹුරා	
Family- **Colubridae**			
02	*Ahaetulla nasuta*	Green Vine Snake / ඇහැටුල්ලා	
03	*Amphiesma stolatum*	Buff-stripped Keelback / අහරකුක්කා	
04	*Atretium schistosum*	Olive Keelback / දිය වර්ණා, කඩොලා	
05	*Boiga beddomei*	Beddome's Cat Snake / කහ මාපිලා	
06	*Boiga forsteni*	Forsten's Cat Snake, කබර මාපිලා, ලේ මාපිලා, නාග මාපිලා	
07	*Ptyas mucosa*	Common Rat Snake / ගැරඩියා	
08	*Chrysopelea taprobanica*	Sri Lanka Flying Snake / ශ්‍රී ලංකා දගරදන්ඩා	
09	*Coelognathus helena*	Trinekt Snake / කටකළුවා	
10	*Dendrelaphis tristis*	Common Bronzeback Tree Snake / තුරු හාල්දන්ඩා	
11	*Xenochrophis piscator*	Checkered Keelback / දිය නයා, දිය පොළඟා	
Family- **Elapidae**			
12	*Naja naja*	Spectacled Cobra / නයා, නාගයා	
Family- **Viperidae**			
13	*Daboia russelii*	Russel's Viper / තිත් පොළඟා	
14	*Hypnale hypnale*	Hump-nosed Pit Viper / කුණ කටුවා, පොලොන් තෙලිස්සා	
Family- **Agamidae**			
15	*Calotes calotes*	Green Garden Lizard / පලා කටුස්සා	
16	*Calotes ceylonensis*	Sri Lanka Painted-lip Lizard / ශ්‍රී ලංකා තොල් විසිතුරු කටුස්සා	
17	*Caltes versicolor*	Common Garden Lizard / ගරා කටුස්සා	
18	*Otocryptis nigristigma*	Sri Lanka Lowland Kangaroo Lizard / ශ්‍රී ලංකා පිනුම් කටුස්සා, ශ්‍රී ලංකා තැලි කටුස්සා	
Family- **Gekkonidae**			
19	*Hemidactylus parvimaculatus*	Sri Lanka Spotted House Gecko / ශ්‍රී ලංකා පුල්ලි ගෙවල් හූනා	
20	*Hemidactylus depressus*	Sri Lanka Kandyan Gecko / ශ්‍රී ලංකා හැලි ගේහූනා	

No	Scientific Name	Common Name	1
21	*Hemidactylus frenatus*	Common House Gecko / සුලබ ගේහුනා	
	Gehyra mutilata	Four-claw Gecko / චතුරන්ගුලි හූනා	
22	*Hemidactylus leschenaultii*	Bark Gecko / කිඹුල් හූනා, ගස් හූනා	
Family- **Scincidae**			
23	*Eutropis carinata lankae*	Common Skink / ගැරඬි හිකනලා / සුලබ හිකනලා	
24	*Eutropis macularia macularia*	Bronzegreen Little Skink / පිහු හිකනලා	
25	*Lankascincus fallax*	Sri Lanka Common Supple Skink / ශී ලංකා සුලබ ලක්හීරළුවා	
Family- **Varanidae**			
26	*Varanus bengalensis*	Land Monitor / තලගොයා	
27	*Varanus salvator*	Water Monitor / කබරගොයා	
Family- **Crocodylidae**			
28	*Crocodylus paluster*	Mugger Crocodile / හැල කිඹුලා	
Family- **Bataguridae**			
29	*Melanochelys trijuga*	Black Turtle / ගල් ඉබ්බා	
Family- **Testudinidae**			
30	*Geochelone elegans*	Star Tortoise / තාරකා ඉබ්බා, මාවර ඉබ්බා	
Family- **Trionchidae**			
31	*Lissemys punctata*	Sri Lanka Flapshell Turtle / ශී ලංකා අළු ඉබ්බා, ශී ලංකා කිරි ඉබ්බා	

Checklist of Birds

No	Scientific Name	Common Name	
Family- **Phasianidae**			
01	*Coturnix chinensis*	Blue Quail / නිල් පිරිවටුවා	
02	*Galloperdix bicalcarata*	Sri Lanka Spurfowl / ශ්‍රී ලංකා හබන්-කුකුළා	
03	*Gallus lafayetii*	Sri Lanka Junglefowl / ශ්‍රී ලංකා වලි කුකුළා	
04	*Pavo cristatus*	Indian Peafowl / මොනරා	
Family- **Anatidae**			
05	*Dendrocygna javanica*	Lesser Whistling-duck / හීන් තඹ-සේරුවා	
06	*Nettapus coromandelianus*	Cotton Pygmy-goose / මල්-සේරුවා	
07	*Anas querquedula*	Garganey / බැමසුදු තාරාවා	
Family- **Podicipedidae**			
08	*Tachybaptus ruficollis*	Little Grebe / පුංචි ගෙඹිතුරුවා	
Family- **Ciconiidae**			
09	*Mycteria leucocephala*	Painted Stork / ලතුවැකියා	
10	*Anastomus oscitans*	Asian Openbill / විවරතුඩුවා	
11	*Ciconia episcopus*	Woolly-necked Stork / පාදිලි මානාවා	
12	*Leptoptilos javanicus*	Lesser Adjutant / හීන් බහුරු-මානාවා	
Family- **Threskiornithidae**			
13	*Threskiornis melanocephalus*	Black-headed Ibis / හිසකළු දැකැත්තා	
14	*Platalea leucorodia*	Eurasian Spoonbill / හැඳිඅලවා	
Family- **Ardeidae**			
15	*Ixobrychus sinensis*	Yellow Bittern / කහ මැටි-කොකා	
16	*Ixobrychus cinnamomeus*	Cinnamon Bittern / කුරුඳු මැටි-කොකා	
17	*Ixobrychus flavicollis*	Black Bittern / කළු මැටි-කොකා	
18	*Nycticorax nycticorax*	Black-crowned Night-heron / රෑ-කොකා	
19	*Ardeola grayii*	Indian Pond-heron / කණ-කොකා	
20	*Bubulcus ibis*	Cattle Egret / ගේරි-කොකා	
21	*Ardea cinerea*	Grey Heron / අළු කොකා	
22	*Ardea purpurea*	Purple Heron / කරවැල් කොකා	
23	*Casmerodius albus*	Great Egret / මහ-කොකා	
24	*Mesophoyx intermedia*	Intermediate Egret / මැදි-කොකා	
25	*Egretta garzetta*	Little Egret / පුංචි අනු-කොකා	

No	Scientific Name	Common Name
Family- **Pelecanidae**		
26	*Pelecanus philippensis*	Spot-billed Pelican / තිත්හොට පැස්තුඩුවා
Family- **Phalacrocoracidae**		
27	*Phalacrocorax niger*	Little Cormorant / පුංචි දියකාවා
28	*Phalacrocorax fuscicollis*	Indian Cormorant / ඉන්දු දියකාවා
29	*Phalacrocorax carbo*	Great Cormorant / මහ දියකාවා
Family- **Anhingidae**		
30	*Anhinga melanogaster*	Oriental Darter / අහිකාවා
Family- **Falconidae**		
31	*Falco tinnunculus*	Common Kestrel / පොදු උකුසුගොයා
Family- **Accipitridae**		
32	*Pernis ptilorhyncus*	Oriental Honey-buzzard / සිළු බඹරකුස්සා
33	*Elanus caeruleus*	Black-winged Kite / කළු උරිස් පතනකුස්සා
34	*Haliastur indus*	Brahminy Kite / බමුණු පියාකුස්සා
35	*Haliaeetus leucogaster*	White-bellied Sea-eagle / කුසඇලි මුහුදුකුස්සා
36	*Ichthyophaga ichthyaetus*	Grey-headed Fish-eagle / අළුහිස් මසුකුස්සා
37	*Spilornis cheela*	Crested Serpent-eagle / සිළු සරපකුස්සා
38	*Accipiter badius*	Shikra / කුරුළුගොයා
39	*Accipiter virgatus*	Besra / බසරා කුරුළුගොයා
40	*Spizaetus cirrhatus*	Changeable Hawk-eagle / පෙරැලි කොණ්ඩකුස්සා
Family- **Rallidae**		
41	*Amaurornis phoenicurus*	White-breasted Waterhen / ළයසුදු කොරවක්කා
42	*Porphyrio porphyrio*	Purple Swamphen / දම් මැදි-කිතලා
43	*Gallinula chloropus*	Common Moorhen / පොදු ගැලිනුවා
44	*Fulica atra*	Common Coot / පොදු කිතලා
Family- **Turnicidae**		
45	*Turnix suscitator*	Barred Buttonquail / බෝල්වටුවා
Family- **Burhinidae**		
46	*Burhinus oedicnemus*	Eurasian Thick-knee / ගොල්-කිරලා
47	*Esacus recurvirostris*	Great Thick-knee / මාගොල්-කිරලා
Family- **Recurvirostridae**		
48	*Himantopus himantopus*	Black-winged Stilt / කළුපිය ඉපල්පාවා

No	Scientific Name	Common Name
Family- Charadriidae		
49	*Vanellus malabaricus*	Yellow-wattled Lapwing / කහ යටිමල් කිරළා
50	*Vanellus indicus*	Red-wattled Lapwing / රත් යටිමල් කිරළා
51	*Pluvialis fulva*	Pacific Golden Plover / සෙත්කර රන් මහ-ඕලෙව්යා
52	*Charadrius dubius*	Little Ringed Plover / පුංචි මාල ඕලෙව්යා
53	*Charadrius alexandrinus*	Kentish Plover / කෙන්ටි ඕලෙව්යා
54	*Charadrius mongolus*	Lesser Sand Plover / හීන් වැලි ඕලෙව්යා
Family- Jacanidae		
55	*Hydrophasianus chirurgus*	Pheasant-tailed Jacana / සැවුල් දියසෑනා
Family- Scolopacidae		
56	*Gallinago stenura*	Pintail Snipe / උල්පෙඳ කැස්වටුවා
57	*Tringa totanus*	Common Redshank / පොදු රත්පා සිලිබිල්ලා
58	*Tringa stagnatilis*	Marsh Sandpiper / වගුරු සිලිබිල්ලා
59	*Tringa nebularia*	Common Greenshank / පොදු පලාපා සිලිබිල්ලා
60	*Tringa glareola*	Wood Sandpiper / වන සිලිබිල්ලා
61	*Actitis hypoleucos*	Common Sandpiper / පොදු සිලිත්තා
Family- Laridae		
62	*Sterna nilotica*	Gull-billed Tern / ගලතුඩු මුහුදුලිහිණියා
63	*Sterna dougallii*	Roseate Tern / අරුණු මුහුදුලිහිණියා
64	*Sterna hirundo*	Common Tern / පොදු මුහුදුලිහිණියා
65	*Sterna albifrons*	Little Tern / පුංචි මුහුදුලිහිණියා
66	*Chlidonias hybrida*	Whiskered Tern / අඟපිය කාගුල්ලිහිණියා
Family- Columbidae		
67	*Columba livia*	Rock Pigeon / පරෙවියා
68	*Stigmatopelia chinensis*	Spotted Dove / අළු-කොබෙයියා
69	*Chalcophaps indica*	Emerald Dove / නීල-කොබෙයියා
70	*Treron bicinctus*	Orange-breasted Green-pigeon / ළයරන් බටගොයා
71	*Treron pompadora*	Pompadour Green-pigeon / රත්බොර බටගොයා
72	*Ducula aenea*	Green Imperial-pigeon / නිල් මහගොයා

No	Scientific Name	Common Name	
Family- **Psittacidae**			
73	*Loriculus beryllinus*	Sri Lanka Hanging-parrot / ශ්‍රී ලංකා ගිරාමලිත්තා	
74	*Psittacula eupatria*	Alexandrine Parakeet / ලබු ගිරවා	
75	*Psittacula krameri*	Rose-ringed Parakeet / රෑන ගිරවා	
76	*Psittacula cyanocephala*	Plum-headed Parakeet / පඬු ගිරවා	
Family- **Cuculidae**			
77	*Clamator jacobinus*	Pied Cuckoo / ගෝමර කොණ්ඩකොහා	
78	*Clamator coromandus*	Chestnut-winged Cuckoo / තඹ‍ල පිය කොණ්ඩකොහා	
79	*Cuculus micropterus*	Indian Cuckoo / ඉන්දු කෝකිලයා	
80	*Cacomantis sonneratii*	Banded Bay Cuckoo / වයිර අනුකොහා	
81	*Cacomantis passerinus*	Grey-bellied Cuckoo / කුසළු අනුකොහා	
82	*Surniculus lugubris*	Drongo Cuckoo / කවුඩුකොහා	
83	*Eudynamys scolopaceus*	Asian Koel / කොවුලා	
84	*Phaenicophaeus viridirostris*	Blue-faced Malkoha / වතනිල් මල්කොහා	
85	*Phaenicophaeus leschenaultii*	Sirkeer Malkoha / පතන් මල්කොහා	
86	*Phaenicophaeus pyrrhocephalus*	Sri Lanka Red-faced Malkoha / ශ්‍රී ලංකා වතරතු මල්කොහා	
87	*Centropus sinensis*	Greater Coucal / ඇටි-කුකුළා	
Family- **Strigidae**			
88	*Otus bakkamoena*	Collared Scops-owl / කරපටි කන්බස්සා	
89	*Bubo nipalensis*	Spot-bellied Eagle-owl / උකුසුබකමුණා (උලමා)	
90	*Ketupa zeylonensis*	Brown Fish-owl / බොර කෙවුල්බකමුණා	
91	*Glaucidium radiatum*	Jungle Owlet / වන උපබස්සා	
Family- **Caprimulgidae**			
92	*Caprimulgus atripennis*	Jerdon's Nightjar / දිගුපෙද බිම්බස්සා	
93	*Caprimulgus asiaticus*	Indian Nightjar / ඉන්දු බිම්බස්සා	
Family- **Apodidae**			
94	*Collocalia unicolor*	Indian Swiftlet / ඉන්දු උප-තුරිතයා	
95	*Cypsiurus balasiensis*	Asian Palm-swift / ආසියා තල්-තුරිතයා	
96	*Apus affinis*	Little Swift / පුංචි තුරිතයා	
Family- **Hemiprocnidae**			
97	*Hemiprocne coronata*	Crested Treeswift / සීඑ රුක්-තුරිතයා	

No	Scientific Name	Common Name	1
Family- **Trogonidae**			
98	*Harpactes fasciatus*	Malabar Trogon / ලෝහවන්නිච්චා	
Family- **Coraciidae**			
99	*Coracias benghalensis*	Indian Roller / දුම්බොන්නා	
Family- **Alcedinidae**			
100	*Pelargopsis capensis*	Stork-billed Kingfisher / මානාතුඩු මහ-පිළිහුදුවා	
101	*Halcyon pileata*	Black-capped Kingfisher / කළු ඉසැසි මැදි-පිළිහුදුවා	
102	*Halcyon smyrnensis*	White-throated Kingfisher / ගෙලසුදු මැදි-පිළිහුදුවා	
103	*Ceyx erithaca*	Black-backed Kingfisher / පෙරදිගු හීන්-පිළිහුදුවා	
104	*Alcedo atthis*	Common Kingfisher / මල් පිළිහුදුවා	
105	*Ceryle rudis*	Pied Kingfisher / ගෝමර-පිළිහුදුවා	
Family- **Meropidae**			
106	*Merops orientalis*	Little Green Bee-eater / පුංචි බිගුහරයා	
107	*Merops philippinus*	Blue-tailed Bee-eater / නිල්පෙඳ බිගුහරයා	
108	*Merops leschenaulti*	Chestnut-headed Bee-eater / තඹල හිස් බිගුහරයා	
Family- **Upupidae**			
109	*Upupa epops*	Eurasian Hoopoe / පොරෝව්වා	
Family- **Buceroidae**			
110	*Ocyceros gingalensis*	Sri Lanka Grey Hornbill / ශ්‍රී ලංකා අළු-කැඳැත්තා	
111	*Anthracoceros coronatus*	Malabar Pied Hornbill / පෝරු කැඳැත්තා	
Family- **Ramphastidae**			
112	*Megalaima zeylanica*	Brown-headed Barbet / පොලොස් කොට්ටෝරුවා	
113	*Megalaima rubricapillus*	Crimson-fronted Barbet / රත් මුණත් කොට්ටෝරුවා	
114	*Megalaima haemacephala*	Coppersmith Barbet / රත්ළය කොට්ටෝරුවා	
Family- **Picidae**			
115	*Dendrocopos nanus*	Brown-capped Woodpecker / බොර ඉසැසි පිරි-කැරලා	
116	*Dendrocopos mahrattensis*	Yellow-crowned Woodpecker / කහසිළු පිරි-කැරලා	
117	*Celeus brachyurus*	Rufous Woodpecker / බොරත් අනු-කැරලා	

No	Scientific Name	Common Name	
118	*Picus chlorolophus*	Lesser Yellownape / හීන් කහ ගෙලැසි කැරලා	
119	*Dinopium benghalense*	Black-rumped Flameback / ගිනිපිට පිළි-කැරලා	
120	*Chrysocolaptes lucidus*	Greater Flameback / ලේපිට මහ-කැරලා	
Family- **Pittidae**			
121	*Pitta brachyura*	Indian Pitta / අවිච්චියා	
Family- **Artamidae**			
122	*Artamus fuscus*	Ashy Woodswallow / අළු වනලිහිණියා	
Family- **Aegithinidae**			
123	*Aegithina tiphia*	Common Iora / පොදු අයෝරාවා	
Family- **Campephagidae**			
124	*Tephrodornis pondicerianus*	Common Woodshrike / පොදු වනසැරටිත්තා	
125	*Coracina macei*	Large Cuckooshrike / මහ කොවුල්සැරටිත්තා	
126	*Coracina melanoptera*	Black-headed Cuckooshrike / කළුහිස් කොවුල්සැරටිත්තා	
127	*Pericrocotus cinnamomeus*	Small Minivet / පුංචි මිණිවිත්තා	
128	*Pericrocotus flammeus*	Scarlet Minivet / දීප්තිරත් මිණිවිත්තා	
Family- **Laniidae**			
129	*Lanius cristatus*	Brown Shrike / බොර සබරිත්තා	
Family- **Oriolidae**			
130	*Oriolus xanthornus*	Black-hooded Oriole / කහකුරුල්ලා	
Family- **Dicruridae**			
131	*Dicrurus caerulescens*	White-bellied Drongo / කවුඩා	
132	*Dicrurus paradiseus*	Greater Racket-tailed Drongo / පිතිපෙඳ කවුඩා	
Family- **Rhipiduridae**			
133	*Rhipidura aureola*	White-browed Fantail / බැමසුදු පවන්පෙන්දා	
Family- **Monarchidae**			
134	*Hypothymis azurea*	Black-naped Monarch / කළු ගෙලැසි රදමාරා	
135	*Terpsiphone paradisi*	Asian Paradise-flycatcher / රැහැන්මාරා	
Family- **Corvidae**			
136	*Corvus splendens*	House Crow / කොළඹ කපුටා	
137	*Corvus levaillantii*	Jungle Crow / කළු කපුටා	

No	Scientific Name	Common Name	
Family- **Paridae**			
138	*Parus cinereus*	Great Tit / මහ ටිකිරිත්තා	
Family- **Hirundinidae**			
139	*Hirundo rustica*	Barn Swallow / අටු වැහිලිහිණියා	
140	*Hirundo daurica*	Red-rumped Swallow / නිතඹ රත් වැහිලිහිණියා	
Family- **Alaudidae**			
141	*Mirafra affinis*	Jerdon's Bushlark / පඳුරු ගොමරිට්ටා	
142	*Alauda gulgula*	Oriental Skylark / පෙරදිගු අහස්රිට්ටා	
143	*Eremopterix griseus*	Ashy-crowned Sparrow-lark / කිරුලෑ බිමිරිට්ටා	
Family- **Cisticolidae**			
144	*Cisticola juncidis*	Zitting Cisticola / ඉරි පවන්සැරියා	
145	*Prinia hodgsonii*	Grey-breasted Prinia / ලයළු ප්‍රිණියා	
146	*Prinia sylvatica*	Jungle Prinia / වන ප්‍රිණියා	
147	*Prinia socialis*	Ashy Prinia / අළු ප්‍රිණියා	
148	*Prinia inornata*	Plain Prinia / සරල ප්‍රිණියා	
Family- **Pycnonotidae**			
149	*Pycnonotus melanicterus*	Black-crested Bulbul / කළු ඉසැසි කොණ්ඩයා	
150	*Pycnonotus cafer*	Red-vented Bulbul / කොණ්ඩයා	
151	*Pycnonotus luteolus*	White-browed Bulbul / බැමසුදු කොණ්ඩයා	
152	*Hypsipetes leucocephalus*	Asian Black Bulbul / කළු පිරි-කොණ්ඩයා	
Family- **Slviidae**			
153	*Orthotomus sutorius*	Common Tailorbird / බට්ටිච්චා	
154	*Acrocephalus dumetorum*	Blyth's Reed-warbler / බලසි පන්රැවියා	
155	*Phylloscopus magnirostris*	Large-billed Leaf-warbler / මාතුඩු ගස්රැවියා	
Family- **Timalidae**			
156	*Pellorneum fuscocapillus*	Sri Lanka Brown-capped Babbler / ශ්‍රී ලංකා බොරග පිරි-දෙමලිච්චා	
157	*Pomatorhinus melanurus*	Sri Lanka Scimitar-babbler / ශ්‍රී ලංකා දෑ-දෙමලිච්චා	
158	*Dumetia hyperythra*	Tawny-bellied Babbler / කුසකහ ලඳ-දෙමලිච්චා	
159	*Rhopocichla atriceps*	Dark-fronted Babbler / වතළුරු පඳුරු-දෙමලිච්චා	

No	Scientific Name	Common Name	
160	*Chrysomma sinense*	Yellow-eyed Babbler / නෙත්කහ තණ-දෙමලිච්චා	
161	*Turdoides affinis*	Yellow-billed Babbler / දෙමලිච්චා	
Family- **Zosteropidae**			
162	*Zosterops palpebrosus*	Oriental White-eye / පෙරදිගු සිතැසියා	
Family- **Surnidae**			
163	*Sitta frontalis*	Velvet-fronted Nuthatch / විල්ලුද යටිකුරිත්තා	
Family- **Surnidae**			
164	*Gracula religiosa*	Hill Myna / සැලළිහිණියා	
165	*Acridotheres tristis*	Common Myna / මයිනා	
166	*Sturnus pagodarum*	Brahminy Starling / බමුණු සැරිකාවා	
167	*Sturnus roseus*	Rosy Starling / රෝස සැරිකාවා	
Family- **Muscicapidae**			
168	*Copsychus saularis*	Oriental Magpie-robin / පොල්කිච්චා	
169	*Copsychus malabaricus*	White-rumped Shama / වන පොල්කිච්චා	
170	*Saxicoloides fulicatus*	Indian Robin / කළුකිච්චා	
171	*Muscicapa daurica*	Asian Brown Flycatcher / බොර මැසිමාරා	
172	*Muscicapa muttui*	Brown-breasted Flycatcher / ලයබොර මැසිමාරා	
173	*Cyornis tickelliae*	Tickell's Blue-flycatcher / රන්ළය නිල්-මැසිමාරා	
Family- **Chloropseidae**			
174	*Chloropsis jerdoni*	Jerdon's Leafbird / ජරදන් කොළරීසියා	
175	*Chloropsis aurifrons*	Golden-fronted Leafbird / රන් නලල් කොළරීසියා	
Family- **Dicaeidae**			
176	*Dicaeum agile*	Thick-billed Flowerpecker / මාතුඩු පිලිලිච්චා	
177	*Dicaeum erythrorhynchos*	Pale-billed Flowerpecker / ළාතුඩු පිලිලිච්චා	
Family- **Nectariniidae**			
178	*Nectarinia zeylonica*	Purple-rumped Sunbird / නිතඹ දම් සුටික්කා	
179	*Nectarinia asiatica*	Purple Sunbird / දම් සුටික්කා	
180	*Nectarinia lotenia*	Long-billed Sunbird / දික්තුඩු සුටික්කා	
Family- **Passeridae**			
181	*Passer domesticus*	House Sparrow / ගේකුරුල්ලා	

No	Scientific Name	Common Name	1
Family- **Ploceidae**			
182	*Ploceus manyar*	Streaked Weaver / පන් වඩුකුරුල්ලා	
183	*Ploceus philippinus*	Baya Weaver / රුක් වඩුකුරුල්ලා	
Family- **Estrididae**			
184	*Lonchura malabarica*	White-throated Munia / ගෙලසුදු වීකුරුල්ලා	
185	*Lonchura striata*	White-rumped Munia / නිතඹ සුදු වීකුරුල්ලා	
186	*Lonchura punctulata*	Scaly-breasted Munia/ළය කායුරු වීකුරුල්ලා	
187	*Lonchura malacca*	Tricoloured Munia / තෙපැහැ වීකුරුල්ලා	
Family- **Motacillidae**			
188	*Dendronanthus indicus*	Forest Wagtail / වන-හැලපෙන්දා	
189	*Motacilla flava*	Yellow Wagtail / කහ හැලපෙන්දා	
190	*Motacilla cinerea*	Grey Wagtail / අළු හැලපෙන්දා	
191	*Anthus rufulus*	Paddyfield Pipit / කෙත් වැරටිච්චා	

Checklist of Mammals

No	Scientific Name	Common Name	1
Family- **Elephantidae**			
1	*Elephas maximus*	Asian Elephant / ඇතා / අලියා	
Family- **Loridae**			
2	*Loris tardigradus*	Sri Lanka Red Slender Loris / ශ්‍රී ලංකා රත් උණහපුළුවා	
Family- **Cercopithecidae**			
3	*Semnopithecus vetulus*	Sri lanka Purple-faced Leaf Monkey / ශ්‍රී ලංකා කළු වදුරා	
4	*Semnopithecus priam*	Grey Langur / ඇලි වදුරා	
5	*Macaca sinica*	Sri Lanka Toque Macaque / ශ්‍රී ලංකා රිලවා	
Family- **Sciuridae**			
6	*Ratufa macroura*	Sri Lanka Giant Squirrel / දඩු ලේනා	
7	*Funambulus palmarum*	Palm Squirrel / ලේනා	
Family- **Muridae**			
8	*Tatera indica*	Indian Gerbil / වැලි-මීයා	
9	*Mus musculus*	Indian House Mouse / ගේ හීන්-මීයා	
10	*Mus booduga*	Indian Field Mouse / වෙල් හීන්-මීයා	
11	*Mus fernandoni*	Sri Lanka Spiny Mouse / ශ්‍රී ලංකා කටු හීන්-මීයා	
12	*Rattus rattus*	Black Rat / පොදු ගේ මීයා	
13	*Madromys blanfordi*	White-tailed Rat / වලිගසුදු වන-මීයා	
14	*Millardia meltada*	Soft-furred Metad / කෙස්මුදු කෙත්-මීයා	
15	*Vandeleuria oleracea*	Asiatic Long-tailed Climbing Mouse / ගස්-මීයා	
Family- **Hystricidae**			
16	*Hystrix indica*	Porcupine / ඉත්තෑවා	
Order- **Lagomorpha**			
17	*Lepus nigricollis*	Black-naped Hare / වල් හාවා	

No	Scientific Name	Common Name	1
Order- Eulipotyphla			
18	*Suncus murinus*	Common Musk Shrew / පොදු හික්-මීයා	
Family- Pteropodidae			
19	*Rousettus leschenaultii*	Fulvous Fruit Bat / බෙරකහ පලා-වවුලා	
20	*Pteropus giganteus*	Indian Flying Fox / මා වවුලා	
21	*Cynopterus sphinx*	Short-nosed Fruit Bat / තල-වවුලා	
Family- Rhinolophidae			
22	*Rhinolophus rouxii*	Rufous Horseshoe Bat / බොරත් අස්ලාඩම්-වවුලා	
Family- Hipposideridae			
23	*Hipposideros ater*	Bicoloured Leaf-nosed Bat / දෙපැහැ පත්නැහැ-වවුලා	
24	*Hipposideros speoris*	Schneider's Leaf-nosed Bat / කෙස්කෙට් පත්නැහැ-වවුලා	
25	*Taphozous melanopogon*	Black-bearded Sheath-tailed Bat / රැවුල්කළු කැපුලුම්-වවුලා	
Sub Family- Vespertilioninae			
26	*Pipistrellus tenuis*	Pygmy Pipistrelle / හීන් කොස්ඇට-වවුලා	
Sub Family- Kerivoulinae			
27	*Kerivoula picta*	Painted Bat / විසිතුරු කිරී-වවුලා	
Family- Felidae			
28	*Felis chaus*	Jungle Cat / වල් බළලා	
29	*Panthera pardus*	Leopard / කොටියා	
Family- Viverridae			
30	*Paradoxurus hermaphroditus*	Common Palm Civet / කලවැද්දා / උගුඩුවා	
31	*Viverricula indica*	Ring-tailed Civet / උරුලෑවා	
Family- Herpestidae			
32	*Herpestes fuscus*	Brown Mongoose / බොර මුගටියා	
33	*Herpestes smithii*	Ruddy Mongoose / රත් මුගටියා / හෝතම්බුවා	
34	*Herpestes viticollis*	Striped-necked Mongoose / මහ මුගටියා	

No	Scientific Name	Common Name	1
Family- **Mustelidae**			
35	*Lutra lutra*	Otter / දිය-බල්ලා	
Family- **Canidae**			
36	*Canis aureus*	Golden Jackal / හිවලා	
Family- **Manidae**			
37	*Manis crassicaudata*	Pangolin / කබැල්ලෑවා	
Family- **Suidae**			
38	*Sus scrofa*	Wild Boar / වල් ඌරා	
Family- **Tragulidae**			
39	*Moschiola meminna*	Sri Lanka Mouse Deer / ශ්‍රී ලංකා මීමින්නා	
Family- **Cervidae**			
40	*Axis axis*	Spotted Deer / තිත් මුවා	
41	*Rusa unicolor*	Sambhur / ගෝනා	
Family- **Bovidae**			
42	*Bubalus arnee*	Wild Buffalo / කුලු මීහරකා	

Notes

Notes

The Field Ornithology Group of Sri Lanka

Founded in 1976 in the Department of Zoology, University of Colombo has as its Objectives;

* **To** bring together persons who are interested in the study and conservation of the birds of Sri Lanka.

* **To** generate interest among laymen and students of natural history in the study and conservation of birds.

* **To** institute, direct and carry out a programme of field study, island wide on various aspects of bird biology.

* **To** establish links with other groups in other parts of the world with similar interest.

Field Ornithology Group of Sri Lanka
Department of Zoology,
University of Colombo,
Colombo 03, Sri lanka.
Tel: +94 11 2501332, +94 11 2592609
Fax: +94 11 2592604
E-mail: fogsl@slt.lk, fogsl1976@gmail.com
Web: www.fogsl.net